I would recommend this book
beginning a teaching ca
vides a highly engaging
throughout, as Erik comr
approach places student
meaningful thinking and
and critical thinking. The c
teaching in a meaningful way, clearly explaining key terms, while the 'little nuggets of wisdom' offer an excellent conduit towards putting these ideas into practice. A great resource to help educators navigate the experiences of working in higher education.

LISA STEPHENSON, COURSE LEADER – MA DRAMA AND CREATIVE WRITING IN EDUCATION, CARNEGIE SCHOOL OF EDUCATION, LEEDS BECKETT UNIVERSITY

Independent Thinking on Teaching in Higher Education is an authoritative book that will be of much value to both new and experienced teachers in higher education, sharing theoretically informed and practically rooted advice on how to plan for better student learning. It offers outstanding accessible guidance for good teaching by drawing on ideas and empirical evidence from practice, and provides thoughtful and wide-ranging analysis of the multiple aspects informing good teaching practice.

Essential reading for anyone concerned with, and committed to, offering high-quality learning experiences to their students.

DR NAMRATA RAO, PRINCIPAL LECTURER IN EDUCATION, LIVERPOOL HOPE UNIVERSITY

This book offers what teachers in higher education want and need: practical support in how to improve their everyday practice. Blair's 'little nuggets of wisdom' give useful tips that can serve as a reminder to those who have been teaching for some time and as a confidence-builder for those who are new to the profession.

Supported by an easy-to-read narrative style, *Independent Thinking on Teaching in Higher Education* is a must for those wishing to give more to their students.

OLIVIA FLEMING, CO-FOUNDER OF OₙₑHE

Independent Thinking on Teaching in Higher Education is both philosophical and practical and Erik's voice of experience comes through in a reassuring manner. Also provided is a selection of useful teaching tools for those who are new to teaching in higher education and as well as those who offer training and CPD within higher education institutions.

The author understands very well that the key to successful encounters in education at any level is engagement: getting students involved and interested. Erik employs many useful analogies and metaphors in this regard that I imagine will be used again and again as the book comes into common usage.

Ultimately, *Independent Thinking on Teaching in Higher Education* offers a very reassuring guide to the important things to consider as one develops their craft as a teacher in higher education.

DR REBECCA PATTERSON, SENIOR LECTURER – EDUCATION (DRAMA), FACULTY OF EDUCATION, MANCHESTER METROPOLITAN UNIVERSITY

INDEPENDENT
THINKING
ON ...

TEACHING IN HIGHER EDUCATION

Erik Blair

FROM THEORY TO PRACTICE

ındependent
thinking press

First published by

Independent Thinking Press
Crown Buildings, Bancyfelin, Carmarthen, Wales, SA33 5ND, UK
www.independentthinkingpress.com

and

Independent Thinking Press
PO Box 2223, Williston, VT 05495, USA
www.crownhousepublishing.com

Independent Thinking Press is an imprint of Crown House Publishing Ltd.

Edited by Ian Gilbert.

The Independent Thinking On ... series is typeset in Azote, Buckwheat TC Sans,
Cormorant Garamond and Montserrat.

The Independent Thinking On ... series cover style was designed by Tania Willis
www.taniawillis.com.

British Library Cataloguing-in-Publication Data
A catalogue entry for this book is available from the British Library.

Print ISBN 978-178135369-1
Mobi ISBN 978-178135370-7
ePub ISBN 978-178135371-4
ePDF ISBN 978-178135372-1

LCCN 2020940862

Printed and bound in the UK by
Gomer Press, Llandysul, Ceredigion

For my mum – who would have probably preferred that I had written a nice storybook!

FOREWORD

The schoolteacher who simply lectures is someone we have all experienced in our school careers. It's easy to challenge – and improve – a teacher who thinks their job starts and ends with the delivery of the facts. As for the subsequent learning of what they've delivered? Well, that's a job for the students. Fortunately, good teachers know these days that their job isn't to teach; it's to ensure that their students learn.

But what about the lecturer who simply lectures? All those of us who have been to university know what that is like too. A large lecture hall. A chalkboard/whiteboard/screen at the front (depending on how old we are). A mass of young faces, pens or keyboards poised, a sense of hush when the main attraction shuffles in and takes his or her place at the front, and off we go. After around an hour of delivery, the clockwork mechanism powering the academic runs down until there's barely enough remaining to get out of the lecture hall before the students come back to life. Repeat.

Now, admittedly, I did go to a traditional Russell Group university in the north-east of England which didn't really have to try that hard. Not only that, this was before the 'bums on seats', free market, pay-as-you-go approach took over the world of higher education, not to mention the transformation of so many old caterpillar colleges into new butterfly universities. Maybe the shift from lecturing to genuine teaching owes its roots to such changes, or maybe it's because there is a new generation of lecturers, teachers, tutors and educators who genuinely like young people and want to be part of an institution that sees them grow and develop as independent thinking adults?

Which is where *Independent Thinking on Teaching in Higher Education* comes in.

With so much known these days about the great teaching that makes for great learning, there is no reason why the lecture theatre, tutor room, seminar group or any variation on a theme in the modern higher education pantheon cannot enjoy the best in teaching and learning as well as the best which has been thought or said.

Of course, the limits of a university's teaching are not limited to its walls these days either. Even before the coronavirus pandemic-induced mega-shift to online learning, many of the world's leading institutions were already making their teaching available everywhere to anyone and for free. Which does tend to rather up the ante when you are competing not just for bums on seats but eyeballs on screens with the very best teaching and the very best universities in the world.

Such a world was brought home to me recently when a head teacher told me of a working-class student from his school who had made it to a university in London. Bumping into him not long into his first year as an undergraduate, the head asked how the young man's lectures were.

'I don't go to them,' was the surprising reply.

Fearing the worst (students from poorer backgrounds, although going to university in greater numbers in England in recent years at least, are also the ones more likely to drop out according to the most recent figures[1]), the head teacher asked why that was the case.

---

[1] E. Busby, *Poorer Students Now Even More Likely to Drop Out of University Than Richer Peers, The Independent* (7 March 2019). Available at: https://www.independent.co.uk/news/education/education-news/university-dropout-rates-students-rich-poor-education-a8812526.html.

'Well, I just find out what the lecture is going to be on and then I find the best person in the world who has lectured on that and watch that recording instead. Why would I get out of bed to attend something that wasn't as good as what I could watch on my laptop?'

Well, duh, indeed.

The quality of your teaching counts – whether that's at school or at university, in a lecture hall of a thousand students, in a smaller classroom or online – for perpetuity. It can mean all the difference between pass or fail, between a poor grade or a great grade, between a lifelong love of your subject or a grudging hoop-jumping, between setting a young person up for life or giving them yet another experience that shouts 'this world is not for me'.

With Erik Blair's book as your guide, you can ensure that your teaching will connect with even more students, influence even more academic careers and transform many, many more young lives.

But you don't need me to lecture you on that.

IAN GILBERT
ROTTERDAM

ACKNOWLEDGEMENTS

I would like to thank everyone who helped bring this book to fruition. Various ideas that make up parts of the book have been shared with, commented on and improved by many colleagues and students. There are too many individuals to name personally, but if you have ever been taught by me or if we have ever worked together, then it is highly likely that you have been part of the development of this book.

I am deeply grateful to all at Crown House Publishing for their support and guidance – particularly Beverley, Louise and Emma, who have impressed me with their thorough, professional insights and eye for detail. Every piece of advice they have given has been valuable and is greatly appreciated.

Teaching in higher education is an iterative process that is improved through enactment, feedback and revision. The same is true of writing. Parts of Chapters 1 and 3 have been reworked from some of my earlier blogs and articles, and I would like to thank the University of West London[1], London School of Economics and Political Science[2] and Optimus Education[3] for their kind permission to reuse this work.

There are two individuals who have been a great influence on me and who, without knowing, are always in the background as I write. I would like to thank Don Smith, who is the constant voice of good conscience at my shoulder –

1 E. Blair, What is a Lecturer? *New Vistas*, 5(1) (2019): 38–42.
2 E. Blair, Mapping the Teaching Environment. *LSE Education Blog* (28 April 2019). Available at: https://blogs.lse.ac.uk/highereducation/2019/04/28/mapping-the-teaching-environment.
3 E. Blair, Different Hefts, Different Expectations. *Learning and Teaching Update*, 39 (2010): 4–6.

reminding me about the power of being positive in the teaching environment. And, most importantly, I would like to thank Angela Francis, who keeps me grounded while simultaneously pushing me to be better.

CONTENTS

CONTENTS

FIRST THOUGHTS

QUESTION EVERYTHING

One of the many mantras in the teaching world is, 'You shouldn't have to reinvent the wheel', but my favourite is, 'Adopt, adapt, reject'. When reading through this book, feel free to steal ideas that might work for you or tweak things to fit your students – and also feel free to reject anything that doesn't work for you. Conversely, don't be so closed-minded that you instantly dismiss new ideas. One of the most common retorts that teachers make when faced with new material is, 'Yeah, that's fine in theory but it wouldn't work with my class.' Try to open up and give it a go – apply the concept to your group and then make a value assessment.

This book is structured around five chapters which explore specific aspects of teaching in higher education. Collectively, these chapters conveniently cover the three areas measured in the Teaching Excellence Framework (TEF): teaching quality, the learning environment, and the educational and professional outcomes achieved by students.[1] The first chapter investigates the nature of higher education – focusing on what we might consider to be the role and function of higher education and the task of teaching within such an environment. Chapter 2 examines the structure of higher education – particularly the structure of teaching within higher education – and highlights the benefit of having a structured approach to planning and practice. Chapter 3 offers insight into the various ways

---

[1] See https://www.thecompleteuniversityguide.co.uk/student-advice/where-to-study/teaching-excellence-framework-tef.

that information flows around the teaching environment and how we can map this flow to better support student engagement and interaction. Chapter 4 focuses on using observation as a tool for teaching enhancement and emphasises that this can be done in a collegial and developmental way. Finally, Chapter 5 highlights the role of reflection and reflective practice – exploring how this is best done in a balanced and structured manner.

At the end of each chapter there are some 'little nuggets of wisdom'. These nuggets cover a wide variety of topics – some are presented as ideas that you can quickly implement in your teaching practice and some are there to stimulate your thinking. There is no one answer presented here; instead, the emphasis is on engagement and reflection. But remember: don't accept what I say just because I have written it down. Please don't hesitate to question my suggestions, but also aim to be open to new ideas.

You may already be asking questions about the word 'teaching' itself. In this book, I have been quite deliberate in discussing teaching in higher education rather than the range of higher education activities undertaken by academic staff. There are many student-facing, educational roles in higher education. Some colleagues are employed as professors, some are tutors, some are readers, some are fellows, some have titles as long as their arm and many have titles that don't really explain what they do at all. This book is aimed at all those who teach in higher education. Recognising that this is a long (and ever growing) list of professionals, and because of the nature of this book, I have preferred to concentrate on what people *do* rather than their job titles.

For example, many people employed in higher education are employed as a *lecturer* and this can lead to some confusion, especially for novice lecturers. The word suggests that what you will be doing is *lecturing,* but that is a rather old-fashioned perspective because to deliver a lecture is a rather specific activity. You may be employed as a lecturer, but try to think about that as your job title rather than as a description of what you do. Individuals who are employed as lecturers undertake many different tasks (as discussed in Chapter 1), but I have focused on one particular task – teaching. Consequently, 'lecturer' is a description of what someone is employed to be, but 'teaching' is what they are employed to do.

For this reason, in this book I refer to the individual doing this teaching as a 'teacher', in order to place the concept of teaching front and centre where I feel it belongs. Some colleagues might be irked by this and regard the term a slight to their academic status; however, that is not my intention. I recognise that all those who teach in higher education have to juggle many different responsibilities. I am simply drawing out one of those roles, teaching, in an effort to shine a light on something that is central to the student learning experience.

It is this emphasis on teaching as an act of doing that is at the heart of this book. The focus is on how we take complicated ideas, theories and concepts and organise them in such a way that they are accessible (and useful) to students – that is, teaching in higher education as a fundamentally person-centred activity.

CHAPTER 1
OPENING THE BEETLE BOX

Before we examine teaching in higher education, we need to think about who it is that does the teaching. By and large, this person is employed as a lecturer, but lecturers are not the only people who teach in higher education – there are also tutors, graduate teaching assistants, fellows, readers and professors, as well as other colleagues who work with students to develop specific skills (both technical and academic). Becoming someone who teaches in higher education (whatever your role or job title might be) 'is not a simple matter, with almost a decade required to prepare an individual for even an entry-level role'.[1] With so much effort involved, it might be worthwhile to find out just what is expected of those who teach in higher education. A quick internet search using terms such as 'lecturer', 'reader' or 'academic support tutor' will provide a surface definition, but this description is likely to be limited in scope – focusing on the duties and responsibilities of someone working in higher education.

In this chapter, I will dig below surface definitions and start to explore the interaction of various personal and professional demarcations. In doing so, I hope to move the conversation beyond a discussion of what someone who teaches in higher education is employed to do and focus on what they actually do.

---

1 H. Coates and L. Goedegbuure, Recasting the Academic Workforce: Why the Attractiveness of the Academic Profession Needs to Be Increased and Eight Strategies for How to Go About This from an Australian Perspective. *Higher Education*, 64 (2012): 875–889 at 876.

DISCIPLINARY ROOTS

Say the word 'learning' and you might get a mental picture. Most people can come up with their own definition of learning, although this is often narrow and prejudiced by personal experience. However, language can change its meaning according to context, therefore the meaning of the word 'learning' is likely to depend on who is using it and the specific conditions in which they find themselves. In his analysis of private and public language, Wittgenstein tells a story of two boys, each with a matchbox containing what he calls a 'beetle'.[2] They agree never to look inside each other's matchbox and also agree that they both contain a beetle. In this analogy, we see that the thing that is 'beetle' is private to each boy and that the term only has meaning on account of its public use. It does not actually matter what is in the box – the word 'beetle' now means 'the thing inside the box'. In a similar way, individuals (lecturers, students and the public at large) discuss the thing inside their head that they call 'teaching'.

Language is also context-bound: the setting for Wittgenstein's example was a game played by two boys, but two zoologists working in the tropical rainforests of Trinidad and Tobago would have a different understanding of 'beetle'. Likewise, the word 'teaching' also has a private meaning, but we can only communicate with others when they share a similar understanding of the word. In this way, language is private-shared – no one person can decide on the 'true' meaning of any term. However, while we might all have our own meanings, in practice they are often not so different and can overlap with the meanings of others. This vast Venn diagram of meaning holds a

---

2   L. Wittgenstein, *Philosophical Investigations* (Oxford: Blackwell, 1953), §293.

practical truth about what 'teaching' actually is (even if this agreed definition is hard to conceptualise or verbalise).

Teaching in higher education is a personally negotiated experience. Individuals will have taken different journeys to arrive at their present situation and will be uniquely shaped by those experiences. However, working within a shared institutional system tends to have a normative effect. Foucault suggests that 'we live inside a set of relations',[3] so any discussion of meaning or interpretation also needs to consider communicated norms within the context of higher education. These norms are the result of, among other things, governmental and institutional directives, student expectations, graduate outcomes, departmental and disciplinary cultures and the assorted needs of various stakeholders. Teaching in the 'supercomplexity' of modern higher education is therefore about much more than simply being an expert within a certain field.[4]

Understanding what it means to teach in this environment involves problematising how we conceptualise learning, examining what we think education is for, questioning our own identity as conduits to knowledge and reflecting on our individual biases. In so doing, we allow the significance of everyday academic roles and regular teaching/learning activities to be examined afresh. Everyone who teaches in higher education has their own approach to teaching, and because everyone who teaches in higher education has had a personal experience of being taught, almost everyone has their own understanding of what it means to teach in this environment (and almost everyone has something to say about teaching).

3 M. Foucault, Of Other Spaces [tr. J. Miskowiec]. *Diacritics*, 16(1) (1986): 22–27 at 23.

4 R. Barnett, *Realising the University in an Age of Supercomplexity* (Maidenhead: Open University Press, 2000).

However, teaching in higher education is not just one easily defined activity. Many individuals develop their conception of their role by engaging with pre-formed ideas about how their subject should be taught and learned – an understanding rooted in their experience of disciplinary learning. These discipline-specific thoughts can be both conscious and unconscious but they tend to be limited in their scope – focusing on the story of how one individual became an expert in one particular aspect of one particular discipline. Furthermore, the philosophical underpinnings of our pedagogy are often individual and disciplinary rather than institutional or universal.

As well as engaging with the knowledge base, those teaching in higher education may have learned the methods, modes and practices of their subject in various ways. For some, their pedagogical approach has been carefully constructed through the scrutiny of educational theory, the critical reading of educational literature and reflective practice. Many develop their practice by studying towards formal higher education qualifications. But there are also a great many people in higher education who developed their teaching practice tacitly and built their understanding of their role through direct on-the-job experience. No matter which route an individual has taken, it is their destination (the higher education institution that employs them) that defines the requirements of their role. These requirements are often outlined in job descriptions, but the tasks actually undertaken when teaching in higher education can also be rather nebulous and difficult to capture. Once we begin to examine the everyday routines of the role, we can begin to capture what it means to be a teacher and from there we can start to scrutinise the rationale behind our activities.

As we have already discussed, an individual's educational journey and experiences will have coloured how they see their teaching role. For some this will mean that they find themselves teaching as they were taught, while others may want to rebel and try new approaches. Those who teach in higher education tend to have studied a particular topic (whether that is physics, economics, film-making or academic writing skills) and their studies are likely to have been embedded in a particular teaching format or 'signature pedagogy'. (A signature pedagogy is the typical way that a specific discipline is taught.) These stereotypical approaches relate to the pedagogy of the subject and to the resources used. For example, it is customary for law to be taught using rote learning and the Socratic approach (where carefully constructed questions lead to logical answers); it is typical for basketball to be taught on the court rather than in a classroom; and if we were to take up parachute jumping, then we would almost certainly expect to get in an aeroplane at some point. Before we even arrive in a higher education learning environment, we need to think about how we have been conditioned by our previous learning.

TEACHER-LED VS. STUDENT-LED PEDAGOGY

Broadly, there are two things we can do in response to our educational conditioning: we can comply or we can rebel. The first is easy and probably doesn't take too much thinking; however, we will simply perpetuate the system. If you were not happy with the way you were taught when you attended higher education, then you need to start rebelling now! Realistically, this might not be the right time to start a revolution, so our rebellion may need to be smaller and more aligned to academic norms. We can begin by being more reflective and more critical – not simply reproducing the established ways but questioning their validity and purpose. Whenever I meet someone who has memorised a poem by heart I am generally unimpressed – remembering lengthy stanzas of poetry is clearly not easy, but it is the application of this learning that is important to me. So, our first reflective acts of rebellion should involve examining the utility of some of the ways our subjects are taught – whether they are taught in a certain way because that is the only possible way to teach them or because of convention. If you can see alternative ways of teaching your topic, then explore these further.

Imagine we were teaching an introductory class on basketball and the focus of the class is how to get the ball into the hoop. There are two main teaching methods we could apply: a *deductive* pedagogy or an *inductive* pedagogy. The deductive approach tends to be teacher-led. It starts with definitions, descriptions and demonstrations. (The way I remember this is that the word 'deductive' starts with the letters 'd' and 'e', as do define, describe and demonstrate.) We would gather the class around and carefully talk them through the various stages of standing, aiming, throwing and scoring a basket. After this structured demonstration, the group would go and practise these skills, and then we would bring them all together in a final plenary during which we would review what they have done and what they have learned.

If we were to adopt an inductive approach, we would start by giving the students two things: (1) the problem we want them to solve and (2) the criteria for success. We would explain that we want them to get the ball in the hoop and that they should find the most consistent method for doing so. We would then send them off to experiment. Our role would be to oversee and take notes, but to be ready to act or to be on hand for any questions that may arise. After experimenting, we would draw the group together and review their success/failure. We would then ask the students to relate what the literature (or coaching manual) suggests to what we, as a class, found to be the most successful approach. Where there are discrepancies we would explore these, and where there are consistencies we would examine why we think that certain approaches worked best. (I remember what 'inductive pedagogy' is because it starts with the word 'in' – and this method usually involves students getting stuck in.)

Both deductive and inductive methods have their strengths and weaknesses, and it is more than likely that our teaching will use a blend of the two. The point is that there is usually at least one other way to teach a topic. If we were to apply deductive and inductive pedagogical methods to the teaching of academic writing – something that most of us in higher education have to teach to some degree – then we might decide to show students what to do (deductive) or we might get them to look at instances of good and bad academic writing and work out some key rules for themselves (inductive). In medicine, we might explain the skeletal features of the human body or we might give each student a bone and ask them to work as a team to recreate the entire skeleton. When teaching film-making, we might talk students through the shots of famous directors, explaining their significance, structure and staging, or we might give each student a five-minute clip and ask them to analyse the narrative structure and share five key points with their peers.

Ultimately, these shouldn't be either/or approaches – the most appropriate learning techniques will probably require you to use a mixture of both inductive and deductive pedagogies. But the decisions behind choosing one approach over another at any given point should not be based on what is 'normally' done, but what you think is the best way of teaching a topic alongside what you think is the best way for your students to learn it.

REMEMBERING INFORMATION IS NOT THE SAME AS USING INFORMATION

Our personal learning experiences often guide how we see our teaching role. Our own teachers may have had a preference for deductive over inductive pedagogy. They may have been inspirational individuals who could capture the attention of their students. They may have been firm but fair. They may have been quiet as a mouse and let the class run riot. Our teachers' pedagogy may have been very obvious to us at the time, such that we might now wish to replicate their teaching style. Or it may be that we were never really aware of their approach to teaching, but we have been immersed in it and now feel that is just the way it is done.

Once we have started to understand why we might be conditioned to teach in a particular way, and considered the different ways we each conceptualise learning, we can begin to do something about it. Through understanding our various pedagogical and personal biases we can start to identify our own previous blind spots. These might include the inability to see the difference between *teaching* and *telling*. This can come about through misremembering our own learning – focusing on the facts, figures and formulas that we now know rather than focusing on how our teachers helped us to learn this information.

Another related blind spot is recognising the difference between *knowledge* and *understanding*. When beginning a teaching career in higher education, many people take a content-led approach. They ask questions such as, 'What do the students need to know?' or 'What is the best order in which to organise the materials?' The reason we ask these questions is because we want to make sure we have fully informed the students, which is terrific. However, by focusing on knowledge retention, rather than on how the students make sense of this new knowledge, we can become overly focused on telling rather than teaching. The trouble with simply seeing learning as a list of information to be remembered is that effective learning involves understanding, and to support this teachers need to make sure that their students are involved in active learning so that they might assimilate this information. Abstract information that is merely 'passed on' to students might not make sense, and if it does not make sense then they are likely to ignore it and move on to other matters. The content-led approach might be time efficient – in that teachers can ensure that everything on the curriculum has been transferred to the students – but unless they are guided to understand this new information, there is a chance that everyone's time has, in fact, been wasted. It is important to think about what we want our students to know, but we also need to consider the processes of learning and of making sense of new material.

Engagement means being involved and interested. Sometimes we learn because we are passionate about something, but this is not always the case. If our students are passionate learners, then our choice of teaching method is less important because they are already driven to learn. It is when our students are not so focused that our teaching choices become even more important. If we move beyond thinking about learning as 'stuff to be remembered' we can support both of these groups. Students who are passionate about a subject will be further invigorated if they can engage with the material in a way that is meaningful and enhances their critical abilities, and students who are not quite so switched on will have the chance to be challenged if they are presented with new approaches, rather than being asked to do the same old thing but with the expectation of a different outcome.

Without challenge and a focus on critical thinking, teaching in higher education can become content driven and (probably) dull. This is not to say that asking students to be active in their learning will automatically lead to better educational outcomes, but doing and learning are clearly linked. The question for those of us who teach in higher education should be: 'What will I ask students to do in order for them to become critical with the topic?' 'Teaching' is a verb, but so is 'learning' – they both involve being active. It is the responsibility of those who teach to create an environment in which activities are organised to inspire and stimulate. Our students are clever people; they will become bored and disillusioned if we stick within the norms of our signature pedagogies.

WHAT IS THE POINT OF HIGHER EDUCATION?

As well as attempting to conceptualise their own role, those who teach in higher education might also take a step back and examine what they see as the purpose of higher education. Some might consider their role to be about the transmission of knowledge, some might see themselves as the co-creators of knowledge, and others will have a less formulated conception. Many people assume they know what the word 'education' means and what it is, but do we all share the same definition or is this another beetle in a box?

Different schools of thought have sprung up around education, but two of the most prominent are traditional and progressive teaching. Traditionalists believe that education should be about teaching for specific or extrinsic aims, often concerned with an individual's function or role in society. All the desks face forward and the person at the front of the room is there to instruct. The students work in silence and they raise their hands to answer questions, not to ask them. Within higher education, the students are taught answers, not processes. Traditional education is about raising individuals who will work for the common good.

In contrast, progressive thinkers believe that education should be about enlightenment, that it has broad aims and is intrinsically worthwhile, that it is about enabling students to grow and meet their true potential. Progressive higher education is connected with self-development, self-fulfilment, self-actualisation and supporting the various aspects of an individual that make them unique.

Both approaches have positives and negatives. Traditional education focuses on developing systems of doing, so it is often criticised for being routine or even boring. However, it is less likely to be corrupted by ideals and is more likely to lead to student employment. Progressive education aims to develop systems of thought that are open-ended and personal. However, if we encourage people to think for themselves, then we must be ready for them to draw conclusions that we may not like.

Beyond all this, we might wish to consider what our students want from education. Attending higher education to learn to be a lawyer, film-maker or economist might involve some narrow activities during which first principles and key skills are taught. Many students appreciate this tangible learning. Others might want to be stretched, to feel inspired and to grow as thinkers. The truth is probably somewhere in-between: students want to learn facts, figures, theories and formulas, but they also want to develop critical thinking skills. This blend of knowledge and understanding will initially make them more employable, but it will also support them to feel able to define their own career path later on. It is the responsibility of those who teach in higher education to support this development, rather than try to impose their own understanding of the nature and role of knowledge – their epistemological perspective. One of the first tasks in higher education teaching, therefore, involves personally negotiating what higher education is, trying to be cognisant of what others might think higher education is, learning to position yourself within this context, and working out how to create a system of learning that does not just repeat the previous system because we can't think of anything better to do.

UNDERSTANDING THE IDENTITIES OF THOSE WHO TEACH AND THOSE WHO LEARN

Humans are social beings who gather together for mutual support, safety and stimulation. Students and those who teach them are also social beings grouped in our own unique ways. These groups are likely to be formed through common interests, needs or desires and created in a socially organic manner. They are also enhanced by identification within a field, such that new professors of English tend to think and act in the same ways as the aged members of their departments. Geologists congregate with other geologists, all thinking geologically. Physicists orbit each other and form specific connections. Those teaching media studies learn to speak through the language of the image.

The philosopher Julian Baggini discusses such groups of people as 'hefts': social groups that are formed through shared ways of being. The term 'heft' comes from the Cumbrian farming practice whereby sheep are not fenced in but learn through the habits of older sheep not to leave their territory:

> *A heft is the unfenced area sheep learn to keep themselves within. This was originally taught to them by shepherds, but as time goes by, they pass it on to each other and need no shepherding. Sheep who learn this are called hefted, and in much the same way, so are people. Their territorial boundaries are more complicated and flexible, but they too rarely stray beyond them, without a shepherd, even though there are no fences keeping them in. Individualism is a great myth. All that has really happened is that we have dispensed with the sheepdogs and have become hefted.[5]*

The codes of a specific heft are shared through transmitted patterns of behaviours (memes) whereby concepts are passed from person to person and replicated at a conscious and unconscious level. Baggini discusses hefts in relation to the sociocultural identity of adults, but nowhere is the hefting of humans more obvious than in late adolescence and early adulthood – the stage when many are ready to enter higher education. Codes are developed through behaviour, ritual and expression and provide students with a social context which offers safety, codes of being and a place to be themselves. From all this we see

---

5   J. Baggini, *Welcome to Everytown: A Journey into the English Mind* (London: Granta, 2008), p. 150.

that a student's identity is constructed by their experiences. Understanding student identity, and understanding how those who teach in higher education develop their own hefted identities, can help us to see that teaching and learning are not objective activities that are undertaken in a social vacuum. Teaching and learning in higher education are very human activities, so thinking about students as individuals who are constantly being invented and reinvented by their circumstances can help us to develop a pedagogy that is based in the realities of being human. Once we start to explore the codes that make us who we are, we can begin to teach in a way that considers how a person might receive a piece of information.

HEFTED SUCCESS

Success is not only a measure of output and it is not always judged externally by educators, through exams, grades and so on. Some hefts will have broad goals and some might embrace nihilistic ambitions; either way, the group will have a general idea of what being successful means to them. These goals will cover hefted expectations of fitting in and hefted targets of what is expected of an individual (in and out of higher education). Gaining approval from others and being part of something bigger seems to offer a certain cachet and is a visual signal that you have been accepted. As educators, we might hope that crossing the threshold into higher education would consist of entry into a new heft – that of 'student'. But hefting is not a rapid process, so those who enter higher education to study will take time to feel that they belong in the student heft.

Ryan suggests that there are three ways that students are influenced by their kindred peers: information exchange, modelling behaviours and the reinforcement of norms and values.[6] These interactions influence individual heft members as they instinctively mirror and counterfeit the actions, speech and expectations of other members. Different hefts influence and reinforce different definitions of success, set out through social interactions within the group, and while these definitions will still need to be balanced against an individual's desire to get a good degree and earn a good living, they are still at play during much of the learning experience itself.

The difficulty within higher education is that outcomes tend to be tightly prescribed and the institutional definition of success tends to be tied to academic attainment. Higher education is suited to the delivery of specific outcomes – such as degrees, certificates, diplomas and doctorates – which are quantitatively assessed. The pressure on those who teach in higher education is therefore to get students to complete their studies with the best qualification possible, rather than to consider the worth of the learning experience. However, students' learning journeys tend to be more nuanced than this would suggest. They might be navigating personal, social and/or financial problems. They might be trying to fit in with new peers. They might be experiencing love for the first time (or being heartbroken for the first time). All of this is part of their wider learning experience and will impact on their studies, but very little of this is taken into account by the higher education institution itself.

It can seem weird that, after working hard to earn the right to enter higher education, some students seem to switch off. Many early career lecturers imagine that their students will be highly organised, focused and driven to be

6   A. M. Ryan, Peer Groups as a Context for the Socialization of Adolescents' Motivation, Engagement, and Achievement in School. *Educational Psychologist*, 25(2) (2000): 101-111.

successful. But the fact is that education is only one aspect of a student's personhood and they will be maintaining many identities and balancing many roles. Students may choose to go into higher education but their background will continue to affect them once they enter. Some young people might feel like imposters in an institution that is not really for them. This might be based on socio-economics, family background or previous educational experiences. The fact that all students who enter higher education have got there on merit is hard for some people to accept because they have been impacted by various elements in their lives to feel about themselves in a certain way. Those who teach in higher education should not be blind to differences that present themselves: between students and their peers, between students and staff. Difference is not something we should try to get over; it needs to be valued.

It is very hard for those teaching in higher education to counter students' established life narratives, but one of the starting points is not to feel that our own story is a blueprint for others. Those of us who become teachers have been lucky in our educational lives. Not necessarily from the start – this 'luck' probably hasn't come without effort and sacrifice – but as we enter higher education, ready to teach others, we find ourselves in a very privileged position. But my educational journey is personal to me – it has been affected by a number of specific factors and so it is not easily generalisable.

When a colleague says something like, 'When I was their age …' I tend to roll my eyes. If there was one easy answer to any of our problems, then none of us would have problems. Those who teach in higher education have been successful but the methodology of our success may not be universal. Perhaps the key lesson is to realise that our students may not have had any interaction with the factors that have guided us, so instead of expecting them to follow the same route we did, we need to understand their actual circumstances and work to establish how we might best help them. We can think of this as a person-centred pedagogy, where we place the individual at the centre of their own learning and work with them to identify the skills they need to develop in order to best access learning.

HEFTED EXPECTATIONS

Individual expectations of success (self-efficacy) allow students to judge their likely ability to perform a task. This personal perspective is influenced by a number of situational variables, and one of the most significant in strengthening efficacy is provided by socially similar others.[7] Here we find heft members influencing the validity of a fellow heftee's beliefs through displays of attitudes and attributes. Bandura reports that the impact of others on 'beliefs of personal efficacy is strongly influenced by perceived similarity to the models. The greater the assumed similarity, the more persuasive.'[8] When it comes to self-efficacy, it makes sense for students to compare themselves to other students who share their code of being rather than to staff. This is the underpinning value of group work: not simply to get a task done, but for students to learn from each other about alternative ways of thinking and completing a task.

---

7 See D. H. Schunk, Self-Efficacy and Academic Motivation. *Educational Psychologist*, 26(3-4) (1991): 207-231.

8 A. Bandura, Exercise of Personal and Collective Efficacy in Changing Societies. In A. Bandura (ed.) *Self-Efficacy in Changing Societies* (Cambridge: Cambridge University Press, 1997), pp. 1-45 at p. 3.

The modelled behaviours of fellow heft members affect a student's beliefs about whether they are capable (or incapable) of meeting the expectations of the curriculum or the learning outcomes of a seminar. This could lead to two main outcomes: either the student might find that their perspective is shared by significant others and is thus validated, or they might discover that other heft members hold alternative perspectives and they may be influenced by these views. An example of this might be a heft member who originally believes that she can't perform a task being convinced that it is, after all, possible by observing a fellow heft member accomplish the same task. (This example shows a positive outcome of increased self-efficacy through interaction with a socially significant other, but the converse is also just as likely.)

The current curricular measure of success in higher education is defined through end-point grades and degree classification. However, because of their past experiences and their present-day situations, some students will not be able to attain the highest degrees. Even with hard work and dedication, their individual circumstances might work against them. Therefore, the institutional definition of success is bound to let some people down: if all students were to embrace this narrow idea of success, then we would have many individuals essentially agreeing to work hard within a system that will eventually label them as underachieving (which is just another word for failure). Why would someone agree to join such a system? Surely it is better for an individual's self-esteem to set targets that are achievable and specific to their own interests. Luckily, while not all students will graduate with a 2:1 or first-class degree, they should still be able to leave higher education feeling satisfied that, despite the odds, they have achieved something important.

It is not just academic 'underachievers' who might find it difficult to sign up to the curricular model of success. Many talented students become disaffected by the curriculum, and their passion for their subject is diminished as it starts to grate against a narrow target-driven syllabus. Hefts don't suffer this restricted consideration of success: within a heft there is a social dynamic and individuals can be part of the process of constructing a model that sets its own unique outcomes – and since the social dynamic of any group is always in flux, such targets are rarely rigid and often intangible. Unlike the institutional model of success, which is imposed on students and leads to certain failure for some, peers within a heft can develop a model of achievement for all members of the group. Thus, a student can have a rich and satisfying experience in higher education by using the available resources to develop individual projects outside their taught course. For example, a student might learn sufficient business skills to become an entrepreneur and only use the institution as a de facto office space, or they might become engaged with a political group or drop out because they have been offered a recording contract.

THERE ARE NO SIMPLE ANSWERS

A higher education institution is one of the few places that different hefts (student and teacher) come together under one roof, but it does not have a single identity and is made up of a collection of hefts. Within higher education we see subject-specific hefts where, for example, the codes of the history department might not reflect those of the biology department. These codes are exposed through geographic location, models of discipline, classroom displays, ethos and academic success rates. These departmental identities draw specific student hefts to specific subjects, which only serve to augment the departmental identity. McKinnon suggests that 'we are all thrice hefted, intimately immersed in environment, social relations and our own physicality and subjectivity'.[9] The fragmented nature of a higher educational institution emphasises these personalised situational factors.

Students are not alone in belonging to specific groups, and many older groups also exhibit specific characteristics.[10] Therefore, it is reasonable to suggest that those who teach in higher education are also members of various hefts. Ultimately, there is a range of student hefts with a range of expectations. These hefts find themselves learning in an environment that is hefted by subjects which are taught by individuals who are influenced by their own past and present hefts. All this takes place within a framework that offers only a narrow definition of success. When we consider that all this occurs in a context of hormones, relationships, new beginnings, debt and growing personal responsibility, it is surprising that students, by and large, do as well as they do. But is there more that can be done to support these hefted individuals?

Clearly, since we are dealing with human beings, there is no simple answer and no magic wand. Being hefted is not a bad thing – fitting in with a group of similar people can be a fantastic feeling. The difficulty arises when a heft finds itself in an environment that does not share its ideas, ideals or expectations. Perhaps, in an effort to address how we might support hefted individuals, we should start by

---

9   K. M. McKinnon, Adoration of the Mystic Lamb. In C. Gigliotti (ed.), *Leonardo's Choice: Genetic Technologies and Animals* (London: Springer, 2009), pp. 215-234 at p. 231.

10 See L. A. Gavin and W. Furman, Age Difference in Adolescents' Perceptions of Their Peer Groups. *Developmental Psychology*, 25(5) (1989): 827-834 at 827.

considering what students want from higher education. Instead of focusing on uniformity of outcome, higher education institutions could concentrate on the need for students to feel that their goals are worthy. The hefted nature of higher education means that it is possible to offer support across a wide range of interests, both curricular and extracurricular. Some student hefts will be drawn to photography or drama; some will enjoy sport, art, craft or design; some will wish to volunteer in the local community; some will want to be MCs or DJs. None of these goals should be seen as being 'outside' of higher education and none of these goals should be considered any more or less valuable than academic success. Higher education institutions are ideally placed to enhance students' self-efficacy, but there is a need for a philosophical change in the criteria for success. Instead of narrow institutional data-driven outcomes being imposed on students, we might consider a model of higher education that allows students to feel successful because they have achieved in the areas that are important to them.

Teaching in higher education is not just about what happens in the classroom or lecture hall. It is also about understanding the role we have in enhancing someone's future. Some development will be academic and some will be social – both matter! Teaching in higher education means reflecting on our role as conduits of knowledge and as co-creators of understanding. The curriculum is often planned with a generic student in mind, but, like all of us, students are complicated individuals. It is not possible for us to teach *every* student according to their needs, but it is possible to appreciate that there is a range of student needs out there. In practice, this means getting to know your students as individuals, learning about the lives of as many students as possible, listening to 'excuses' without assuming they are playing the game, and constantly reflecting on how your students will learn rather than what you will teach.

When you start teaching in a new higher education institution, you only have a couple of years before you start to fit in. This has its pros and cons. It is reassuring when you work out the ins and outs of your role, when you build good relationships with colleagues, when you start to know your way around institutional policies and procedures, and when you feel like your teaching is making a difference. The downside is that you stop asking questions about your environment. If we place ourselves in our students' shoes, however, we quickly learn that they are asking questions of the higher education environment all the time, and each new cohort enters higher education with their own questions. Fitting in takes us further from the student experience and further from understanding how they might be negotiating this new environment. In order to counter our own institutionalisation, we need to try and see the world through the eyes of our students – talking to them, listening to what they have to say, valuing their perspectives.

It is important to question everything and to move away from the idea that simply because we teach something, then it will be learned. Learning is an active meaning-making process which is undertaken through a hefted framework of understanding. If our teaching practice is based on a model of simply passing on information, then we ignore the unique qualities of our students. It is essential that we help them to understand the literature, theories and first principles of our subject, but in order to create new knowledge (one of the core jobs of higher education), we also need to ask them to filter this through their own experiences by giving them learning activities that challenge them to make sense of facts in relation to their own perspective.

THREE CHALLENGES

1 **Try to see the world through the students' perspective.** When you enter an empty classroom try sitting in some student chairs. Are the chairs comfy? Will the light be shining in their eyes? Will they be able to see their classmates? Will they have a good view of the board you will be working on? Seeing the world through their eyes is a two-part process: it will involve understanding their outlook on life and learning, and understanding their everyday lived experiences. Put yourself in their shoes mentally and physically and try to gain some insight into what learning looks like from their perspective, rather than conceptualising learning as something emitted from the front of the room. Try to remember how different your world is from that of your students. Teaching is much more than the transmission of knowledge. Your job is to inspire, intrigue, motivate, initiate, facilitate and celebrate. Taking time out to sit where they sit and imagine what their experience of learning might feel like may help you to develop a sense of kinship. Rather than regarding students as the recipients of wisdom, aim to consider them as active co-conspirators in the development of knowledge.

2 **Try to focus on the learning process rather than the teaching process.** Instead of asking, 'What will *I* teach?', try asking, 'What will *they* learn?' This simple twist will help to keep you focused on the importance of student engagement. For proactive, on-task and interacting students, focus on helping them to develop critical thinking skills rather than simply throwing facts at them. If teaching is overly deductive then students won't get a chance to make sense of things from their own perspective. Remember that

learning is a verb – a doing word. Instead of telling students that they need to know something, try giving them three positive reasons for learning it. Try to make sure that your students are active learners rather than passive recipients. Our job is not to simply tell students facts and figures but to give them the skills to pick apart the information we share with them – so don't stuff your class full of content. In the age of the internet, facts and figures are less important than skills, attitudes and critical thinking. If we cut down on teacher-talk we might leave more space for learning. When teachers talk less, students talk more. Teachers who focus on providing content reduce student autonomy because the students consequently learn to constantly refer back to the teacher for the 'right' answer.

3 **Try to be measured in the amount of learning support you offer.** When you over-help someone they can become over-reliant on you. Consider under-helping your students – making them work for it. When we spoon-feed information to students, we do the work for them. We rob them of the benefits of rigorous learning. We rob them of effort. We rob them of productive struggle. We rob them of opportunities to develop grit, perseverance and resilience. Give students support, but also give them challenge and let them find their own answers. Instead of showing students how to do something, ask them to discover three possible ways to do it. Then ask them to work together with their peers to find the 'best' way. It is more important for students to think about questions than to simply recite their teacher's answer. Students need to be reminded that it is OK to try new approaches and that making mistakes is an important part of learning. Education is not the gift of

knowledge, it's the gift of enquiry. Getting students active and interactive increases the likelihood of engagement and helps them to take ownership of their own learning. So, fight the urge to intervene. Stay in the background – ready to support when needed – and focus on giving the students problems to work through for themselves.

LITTLE NUGGETS OF WISDOM

TEACHING

- The 'right' pedagogy is the one that is right for your students.

- Pedagogy isn't simply how you teach; it's how you think about the movement from 'knowing something' to 'knowing more'.

- Part of your job is to make difficult knowledge seem achievable with effort.

- Successful learning is not just about a student's commitment to learn; it's also about your commitment to give them something worth learning.

- You are not teaching if no one is learning.

LEARNING

- There is a huge conceptual difference between 'the students in my class' and 'the learning in my class'.

- Learning and knowing are not the same thing – and neither are teaching and telling.

- Students may not be well versed in pedagogy but they know innately many critical things about what supports the learning process.

- All student tasks have two outcomes: what was found (the answer) and what was learned (the skills developed as a result of doing the task). Focus on the latter.

- Everything in education is in the present continuous tense: nothing will ever be truly *learned* as we are all still learning. Students won't suddenly just become autonomous learners – they need us to create an environment of empowerment.

KNOWING

- Knowledge isn't black and white – it's grey. Anyone who claims to know the full answer is deluded. Anyone who claims to know nothing is also wrong.

- Try not to mistake 'knowing what' for 'knowing how'. And remember that real learning involves 'knowing why'.

- In the best classrooms everyone feels comfortable enough to admit to not knowing the answer to a question.

- Never assume that you are the cleverest person in the room. Whether you are teaching 5-year-olds or 50-year-olds, there is always a nugget of wisdom waiting to be discovered.

- Abstract knowledge isn't much use without the development of skills and understanding.

CHAPTER 2

THE STRUCTURE OF TEACHING IN HIGHER EDUCATION

If attempting to find sense in the balance between meaning, perspective, politics and our own place in history is not hard enough, then we might also consider that the jobs undertaken by higher education professionals are not fixed commodities. Kinser discusses how the various aspects that make up the perceived academic role have been 'unbundled', so that tasks which once belonged together and were the responsibility of one individual have now been parcelled out to people with more expertise in certain fields.[1] Among the drivers of this fragmentation are rapidly changing workforce demographics, the repurposing of certain higher education institutions and a movement towards more hybrid forms of teaching, learning and research.[2] Therefore, academic institutions have had to refocus and academic tasks have had to be rethought.

Teaching has been impacted by two structural aspects: firstly, the way that the roles of those who teach in higher education have been organised, and, secondly, the way that these individuals manage their own teaching. To make sense of this world, individuals need to understand their place within the ecosystem and then, once they have established their position, to recognise the power they

---

1   K. Kinser, Working At a For-Profit: The University of Phoenix. *International Higher Education*, 28 (2015): 13-14.
2   Coates and Goedegbuure, Recasting the Academic Workforce.

might have in crafting learning activities within this environment. Archer observes:

> *Academia is a contested territory that entails constant struggles over the symbols and boundaries of authenticity … In other words, questions of authenticity and legitimacy are central to the formation of social relations within the academy – with individuals and groups competing to ensure that their particular interests, characteristics and identities are accorded recognition and value.*[3]

The university is not one unified body, rather it is hefted – made up of academic tribes and territories.[4] The unbundling of roles means there is no longer a simple binary division of academic and non-academic; instead, roles are blurry around the edges. In navigating their way through this new environment, individuals find that their responsibilities are contested rather than fixed, and the old hefts that were formed around departments, disciplines and faculties are now fragmented.[5] This means that the concept of 'teaching' in higher education has become much harder to define because many of us are teaching students for different reasons and with different areas of focus. In practice, this means that someone employed as a lecturer in a history department is just as likely to be working with colleagues from departments focused on supporting students with academic writing as they are to be working with fellow historians.

---

3   L. Archer, Young/er Academics' Constructions of 'Authenticity', 'Success' and 'Professional Identity'. *Studies in Higher Education*, 33(4) (2008): 385–403 at 386.

4   T. Becher and P. Trowler, *Academic Tribes and Territories: Intellectual Enquiry and the Cultures of Disciplines*, 2nd edn (Maidenhead: Open University Press, 2001).

5   E. Blair, Rebundling Higher Educational Research, Teaching and Service. *Confero*, 6(1) (2018): 35–54. Available at: http://www.confero.ep.liu.se/contents. asp?doi=10.3384/confero.2001-4562.1861.

We can see this in the division of the university workforce and the growing number of people who have roles that focus on one particular element of the three key aspects of higher education: teaching, research and administration. For some, this trinity was always a matter of tension as they tried to navigate all three positions, some of which they did not feel equally comfortable in, so the segregation of roles has allowed them to focus on areas of particular strength. For others, this division has been seen as a weakening of their academic autonomy. This shift has led to gaps and overlaps in teaching within higher education, and there are many grey areas. For someone new to a particular institution, their job description might suggest that they will be doing X, Y and Z, but the day-to-day reality might be somewhat different.

THE STRUCTURE OF HIGHER EDUCATION

According to Elkington and Lawrence, new iterations of institutional structures and the uncertainty of academic identity have led to a 'disruption of expectation and inconsistencies in the personal projects of academic staff'.[6] For those who have been involved in higher education for some time, this blurring of roles and the unbundling of academic practice may have given rise to feelings of personal insignificance and a sense of disengagement, especially within the teaching environment.[7] For example, a graduate teaching assistant clearly has a different role

---

6   S. Elkington and L. Lawrence, Non-Specialism and Shifting Academic Identities: A Sign of the Times? *Innovations in Education and Teaching International*, 49(1) (2012): 51–61 at 59.

7   S. Briggs, Changing Role and Competencies of Academics. *Active Learning in Higher Education*, 6(3) (2005): 256–268.

than that of a professor, but over the course of one semester both may find themselves teaching the same class. What does this mean for the assumed hierarchy of graduate teaching assistants and professors, when one might know significantly more than the other about the field itself but the other may be much better at teaching it?

Higher education institutions are not only structured in a hierarchical manner. There are also hazy boundaries between those who teach the subject matter itself and those who teach students skills such as writing for academic purposes or who run workshops aimed at developing information literacy. Where once upon a time a student who did not know how to format references was left to flounder, we now have colleagues who can teach them these skills. This means that the student is no longer hampered by their legitimate ignorance of the technical know-how of academia and is supported to learn such skills as part of a more holistic learning experience. Macfarlane considers this unbundling of higher education to be damaging to the established wisdom of what it means to work within this environment and reports that it has led to a 'two-directional flow of professional support and academic staff into new para-academic roles'.[8] In practice, the tasks undertaken by one lecturer in one institution may be divided and shared among the professional and academic staff in a different institution. This disparity might also occur within the same institution, with job roles similar but different depending on departmental needs. Finding your place in the system can be tricky within such a fluid environment.

The task of teaching in the field of higher education has become harder to categorise due to role fluidity, multiple interpretations of what education might be, personally

---

8   B. Macfarlane, The Morphing of Academic Practice: Unbundling and the Rise of the Para-Academic. *Higher Education Quarterly*, 65(1) (2011): 59–73 at 63.

negotiated definitions of teaching, and inconsistencies in what universities are for. The function of the modern university exists in a state of flux, and is affected by factors such as finance and funding, government policy, employers' needs and student expectations. This movement had led to increased ambiguity in higher education teaching roles, which are now locally rather than globally defined. As we have seen, academic work has historically involved teaching, research and administration, but under each of these headings lie a multitude of tasks that range from photocopying to revenue-raising. Such a breadth of activity means that it is hard for one individual to truly understand their role, let alone for there to be a common conception of various institutional activities and identities.

This is not to say that finding your place in the system is a fruitless task. After a certain amount of time in any job, things begin to settle down and the structure of the institution becomes evident; however, taking time to get to know the lie of the land is an important aspect of teaching. I always recommend that new colleagues take their time to explore the campus, go into lecture halls, visit the campus coffee shops, meet as many people as possible, ask questions, stick their nose in and work out how they fit into their new surroundings.

Many managers take new colleagues on a mini tour of the institution on their first day and introduce them to a whole series of individuals (whose names they instantly forget). One of the reasons they do so is because established members of staff appreciate just how interconnected the higher education environment is. However, after this tour, new members of staff quickly become department-centric and stick within a restricted environment – focusing on preparing for their own individual part in the learning process. It is only later on that they realise why their manager introduced them to Barney in learning resources: because Barney is teaching their students the skills of writing a literature review and this will impact directly on their own teaching module. New colleagues then slowly start to expand their universe and see how they are part of an overall structure with many component parts working in (relative) harmony to support students' learning.

By spending time wandering through the institution's corridors and reviewing its policies and documents in our first few weeks of a new job, we can start to see how the whole system works and we can get a better idea of the specifics of our role within the organisation. Once we have found our personal place in the structure of higher education, we are better positioned to shape our teaching activities within it. Knowing your space means knowing how to act in your space.

THE BENEFITS OF KNOWING THE STRUCTURE

Some aspects of theatrical productions drive me mad. Basically, I know very little about theatre but I have managed to separate it into two groups: plays when I know the end has come and plays when I don't! Shakespeare productions and whodunnits are in the former group – I can see the performance has come to a climax because the murderer has been identified or the cast are lying dead on the stage. The second group are the ones that send me round the twist. We get to what I think is the end … but I'm not sure if it is. Perhaps all the characters freeze, perhaps a main character delivers a mournful monologue then stares off into space, perhaps the lights just suddenly go out. I ask myself, 'Is this the end?' and 'Should I clap now?'

I'm uncertain, so I sit and wait. Hopefully someone else starts the applause (I imagine this person is somehow connected with the theatre company) and then we all join in.

The best production I have ever seen (according to my naive dualistic segregation of drama) was *Oedipus Rex*. I won't tell you the story (and don't ask your mother for a precis) but the structure is perfect. A group of characters known as the chorus walk onto the stage and tell you what the play is about and what you will see. Then the main part of the play happens. Then the chorus return to the stage and describe what you have just witnessed. There is a very clear three-part structure, with a beginning, middle and end, which is shared with the audience. This means that we can concentrate on the content.

The reason I like this format is to do with the comfort it gives me – I feel assured that there is a framework in place. I don't have to worry about surprise endings either. I like this sort of structured approach as a teacher too. Firstly, if I always organise my teaching around a model that I feel will work for me and my students, there is less for me to engineer each time I teach a new topic. I simply have to fit the subject matter into my pre-existing framework. Secondly, having a template for my teaching enables me to see that any teaching event will have at least three phases, and each of these phases will allow for a different type of teaching and learning. Consequently, before I even embark on a new subject, I know that my one-hour class will not be a one-hour lecture. I'm sure that my students are thankful for this; they also like predictability. Just as the three-part play permits me to understand the context of a performance, so the three-part teaching structure enables students to understand what is going on. Knowing your space means knowing how to teach and learn in your space.

THE THREE-PART TEACHING STRUCTURE

If teaching has a clear beginning, middle and end then students are better able to focus on the content. Obviously, in higher education there is a timetable which tells everyone when things will start and end, but what really matters is the way that such events are signalled and the ingredients that constitute them. A three-part seminar is not only useful in arranging the teaching so that students feel they are learning within an organised framework, but it is also a great planning tool which allows those who teach in higher education to work within a purposeful structure. Colleagues need not feel restrained by such an approach; instead, they may wish to consider the benefits of having a predefined system. Let me explain with the help of crabs, jellyfish and humans ...

Crabs have exoskeletons which constrain their growth and offer little flexibility. Jellyfish have the opposite problem – they have gelatinous bodies which are constantly in motion and impacted by external forces. Humans have an endoskeleton – our spines are on the inside. An endoskeleton gives us flexibility within certain planes of movement, it lets us grow and it keeps our internal organs in place. Using a three-part approach to teaching in higher education is akin to having an endoskeleton. There is structure and organisation, but individual teachers also have the ability, during the teaching session itself, to make suitable changes that they feel are appropriate. This is very different from what some might call 'winging it', where there is no structure at all.

The endoskeleton limits an individual's capacity to wander too far off topic as they know they need to be ready for the next phase of the seminar. In this way, the spine gives us both stability and flexibility (within reason). What is more, the endoskeletal three-part structure offers a form that is familiar to students, supporting them to feel comfortable in the knowledge that the work is planned and purposeful. I am not proposing that we organise our teaching by cramming loads of information into the allotted time (which would seem like a waste when all the information is already available on the internet and in the library). Instead, the structure of teaching should be formed through a series of phases, each one building on the previous phase and all coming together in a logical manner.

The three-part structure also helps to highlight what is possible within a teaching session and reduce the potential for the over-stuffing of content. When I plan a seminar, I allow seven minutes at the start for settling in and sharing what is going to be taught/learned. I then teach (which is usually a series of student-led learning events). Finally, I use the last five minutes to review what we have done/learned. Not all colleagues are comfortable with this approach, often because they are working within a content-driven model and feel the need to pack the seminar with as much information as possible. It is important to remember that it is not our job to teach the students everything! It is our job to inspire, provoke intrigue, offer insights, share examples and arouse interest; it is the job of our students to learn.

The three-part structure provides a scaffold for teaching knowledge, skills and understanding in a phased and coherent manner. Setting aside some time at the start of a seminar to review what is to be taught/learned helps the students to feel comfortable and ready to learn, but it also encourages them to see how concepts link together. Likewise, taking some time at the end to review the learning helps to reinforce cognitive linkages so that what has been learned is not seen as a series of separate pieces of information but as a structured whole.

Some teachers might feel that the three-part approach will limit their individuality and freedom. And it might. But that doesn't mean we shouldn't consider it. Teaching, like every other job, has some hoops through which we must jump and some shared wisdom to which we should be open. Higher education is an evidence-based world, so instead of working from our gut instinct or trying to replicate the pedagogy of our own teachers, we should instead look for answers in the research base. Professor John Hattie, director of the Melbourne Education Research Institute at the University of Melbourne, is a man who likes meta-analysis. In fact, his work involves meta-analyses of meta-analyses. He has built up a data set of over 1,200 meta-analyses that examine what actually makes a difference in education. From this work he can assess the effect size of almost any educational intervention – for example, homework and single-sex schooling have almost no effect on learning, while classroom discussion and teacher credibility have a large effect size. From his work on higher education, Hattie reports that some of the strategies that make the biggest difference involve sharing learning intentions (what is to be learned) at the start, having a clear scaffold around learning events and giving meaningful feedback (what has been learned).[9] Personally, I would like Hattie to turn his eye to examining theatre, but in the meantime I'm happy to be guided by the data and stick with the three-part structure.

Whatever teaching format you are using – lecture, seminar, lab work, fieldwork and so on – the three-part structure works. It gives teaching a beginning, middle and end, and avoids individuals thinking that their job is to fill up the allotted time with teacher-talk. Instead, we should be

---

9   J. Hattie, The Applicability of Visible Learning to Higher Education. *Scholarship of Teaching and Learning in Psychology*, 1(1) (2015): 79–91.

filling the various phases with learning activities. At the end of Chapter 1, I observed that one of the first tasks for anyone teaching in higher education is to negotiate what higher education is, so they can teach in a way that is focused on learning rather than just repeating the established pedagogy. In this chapter, I have developed this further to include the structure of higher education and how understanding the system might place an individual in a more comfortable place from which to plan their new pedagogy. For me, systems are not necessarily restrictive: they offer a framework within which we can orchestrate learning. The teaching environment has a physical structure – walls, doors, desks and so on – and our understanding of this space impacts on how we bodily negotiate our way through it. The same is true of the non-physical structure of higher education. Knowing how to negotiate your way through this terrain is a good way of feeling grounded in your environment and establishing a position from which you will be better able to plan teaching that is focused on learning as a sequential and structured event.

TYPES OF TEACHING

Although I have advocated that teaching should have a three-part structure, I also know that, depending on the subject matter, there are different class set-ups. Not all learning involves rows of desks all facing the front – hopefully, hardly any sessions will take this form. Nowadays, typical classroom seating is often arranged in groups or horseshoes; zoologists might be teaching in the field; IT trainers might have banks of students facing computers; and, thanks to technology, distance learning means that students do not even have to be in the same room/town/country as the person teaching them.

What is important is that we have the right set-up to meet our students' needs: if you walk into a room and the desks are not arranged in the way you want them, move them! Of course, we might not have the time or capacity to be repeatedly moving furniture, but the principle still stands – as far as possible we should try to make the physical environment as best suited to the learning as possible. When teaching in a seminar room, for example, we can make some quick physical changes by asking the students to organise themselves into standing groups in the corners of the room, or to arrange themselves in a line-up showing levels of agreement with a topic statement, or, as they enter, to sit next to someone they have not worked with before. When teaching in a large lecture theatre everything is likely to be bolted to the floor, but there is nothing to prevent us from inviting groups of students onto the stage or asking them to discuss a point for a few minutes with the person sitting next to them.

As well as the physical learning environment, we might also wish to consider how we each conceptualise our role in relation to student learning. For example, do you think of your role as a leader, an instructor or a facilitator? Do you see yourself as the source of all knowledge or as someone who is responsible for encouraging students to find out knowledge for themselves? Some insight into these questions can be found by thinking about the word 'delivery'. This is one of those words that is often used in an uncritical way in higher education where people talk about 'delivering a lecture' or 'delivering the curriculum'. For a long time, I had some issues with delivery because it didn't sound like the type of higher education teaching that I wanted to be involved in. But a wise colleague helped me out by offering two metaphors for thinking about delivery (which link to the inductive and deductive pedagogies discussed in Chapter 1).

The first metaphor is the postal worker. The job of the postal worker is to take an item and pass it on to the correct person without tampering with the item itself. As a metaphor for teaching in higher education it is potentially quite powerful. However, it narrows the role of teacher to that of a conduit of knowledge: the person doing the teaching has little agency and simply takes the pre-existing canon of knowledge, repackages it into learnable bites and passes it on to the students. Two things upset me about this model. Firstly, it relegates the person doing the teaching to that of a content provider. Secondly, as someone who has been involved in trying to enhance teaching in higher education for quite some time now, I have seen a lot of this type of teaching. It involves individuals filling PowerPoint slides with copious amounts of information and then reading these slides to their students. The postal worker pedagogue is alive and kicking in higher education, but they should be curtailed as this form of teaching is inefficient and ineffective.

The second metaphor of delivery is the midwife. In this model, the role of the teacher is not to 'tell' their students the answers but to set the conditions for ideas to gestate – the students are charged with creating their own understanding. In this way, teaching in higher education is not simply about passing on information; it is about supporting students to develop the critical skills needed in order to create new knowledge. Our students are bright and in need of inspiration. Postal delivery has its place in helping them to become aware of core knowl-edge, but the midwife model offers them a genuine sense of empowerment.

TEACHING ONLINE

As well as teaching in the physical domain, a great deal of teaching in higher education now happens online. Some colleagues may conceptualise this as a very different type of teaching; however, it is important to remember that the main difference between online and face-to-face teaching is the mode, not the underlying principles. Therefore, the types of questions that underpin successful online teaching are, 'What will I get the students to do?', 'How will I structure my teaching?' and, 'How will my students experience this learning event?' Throughout all this, online teaching should remain an active experience – where the focus is on helping students to feel involved and ready to engage in the learning experience.

Higher education institutions tend to teach using virtual learning environments (VLEs). There are many forms of VLE and they come with add-ons, plug-ins and extensions. For the novice, there is no need to wade deep into this water as the basic VLE will have all that is needed. But for those who are keen, and like to experiment, there is so much to explore. Much like the first step in teaching in the face-to-face environment, the first step in using a VLE is to understand the structure. In understanding the online structure, the component parts are worth investigating, to see what happens where. A typical VLE will have a space for announcements, a space for live teaching (often called synchronous activity), a repository of resources (for asynchronous activity), chat rooms or forums, and a space for assignments to be uploaded, assessed and marks posted. There will be times when we are asked to upload something; there will be times when we interact with our students, and there will be times when we download things (usually assessment-related materials). Virtual learning environments are made up of component features with specific functions, but it is only when the various parts come together that the whole package begins to make sense. In the same way that we might wander the corridors of a higher education institution in order to orientate ourselves, it is a great idea to wander around a VLE. Personally, as I wander around a VLE, I take notes and create a brief glossary that explains to me what each component part does, what I might do with it, and how it relates to another feature that I have reviewed.

Beyond the practical workings of learning to teach online, the more fundamental question of what is to be taught needs to be considered. Because of the nature of online teaching, there is a tendency to overstuff learning activities. When teaching online, the teacher is forced to plan at a distance – in isolation from their students. The main interaction might be between the teacher and their laptop, and this might mean that their thoughts about learning could potentially become less person-centred. With this enforced isolation there is a danger that the teacher starts to focus on trying to ensure that all the material is 'covered' and that the best way to do this is to 'deliver' it in a rather teacher-centred (postal) manner. In this way, online teaching can become overly deductive with the teacher posting great swathes of content and simply expecting students to engage with it. But the principles of effective teaching in higher education are the same online as they are offline – the act of teaching is to support the act of learning, and the best way to do this is by creating situations where students are challenged to make sense of the world around them.

The wider online world already has all the facts and figures that might be needed, meaning there is little need for teachers to spend too much time reconfiguring this knowledge for their VLE. Once we realise that knowledge is already 'out there' we can start to focus on developing online activities that encourage meaning-making and turn our attention to developing critical and cognitive skills. Teaching is about imparting knowledge, skills and understanding. The online environment is already knowledge-rich, so teaching online has to be more focused on supporting the development of skills and understanding.

The skills that will be developed are likely to be critical thinking skills – skills such as judgement, synthesis, analysis, evaluation, creation and categorisation. Instead of asking our students to simply read information, we should help them develop critical thinking skills by asking them to critique something or create something – both of which are possible online. When it comes to developing understanding, this might seem trickier online (and it probably is). The concept of 'understanding' is underpinned through connections and communications and things such as empathy, sympathy and perspective. It is easier to engage with these concepts in the face-to-face world but, online, we can still ask students to try to make cognitive connections – it is just that some of these connections are likely to be more introspective. This means that the development of understanding in the online environment is about giving students the opportunity to reflect on their connection with new concepts. After each phase of learning, we might get them to write a reflective blog or record a two-minute video diary entry in which they reflect on how a new piece of information fits with their established ideas. We could also ask them to reflect on what this information might mean to other people and how others might interpret the same information from a very different perspective.

When teaching online, we should try to examine how asynchronous and synchronous activity can best support the development of knowledge, skills and understanding. It might be easy just to decide that activities undertaken in a student's own time (asynchronous) should be about grounding them in a subject, and that live, face-to-face class webinars (synchronous) will be where the critical thinking will be developed and knowledge applied. But a better model would be to encourage students to be independent critical thinkers, independent knowledge creators and independent artefact designers in both asynchronous and synchronous activity. Many who teach in higher education seek to develop autonomous students – we can't do this by spoon-feeding knowledge in one place and then showing students how to apply it in another. Both asynchronous and synchronous online teaching need to move through phases of 'define', 'do' and 'review'.

It is OK to post narrated PowerPoints, video clips and articles to be read but these types of activity tend to be best for grounding students in a topic. The important thing to remember is that this grounding needs to be built upon, and students need the chance to develop their own ideas and examine the concepts that are presented to them. Good asynchronous learning activities move beyond the consumption of knowledge and challenge students to create artefacts, upload vlogs, write journal entries, produce case studies, engage in group projects and post on discussion boards. Live webinars (synchronous) can also be used to blend knowledge consumption, knowledge critique and knowledge creation – through group work, idea sharing, student-led questioning, quizzes, and peer assessment. The things that make a good online webinar are the same as those that make a good face-to-face seminar: engagement and interaction.

There are some practical things that we can do to support students when teaching online. During webinars, I try to keep my webcam on as much as possible, so that students get a sense that I am a 'real' person, not just a disembodied voice coming through the speakers on their laptop. I also open the webinar 'room' 15 minutes early and close it 15 minutes after the timetabled end of the session. And during this time, I encourage students to have their mic and cameras on, so they can see each other and interact. Likewise, when students present work (individual, paired or group) they should have their cameras on. But humanising online learning isn't just about seeing each other's face – we can try to encourage students to use the chat functions – blending written comments with emojis, GIFs and memes. This type of posting has a normalising effect – it says that learning online still follows the established codes of general online activity. The chat function is also a great tool for identifying student insight and working to develop it – so you can see when a student posts a great point and you can pause and say, 'Wow, Julio just posted a fantastic comment! Can we all scroll back, read Julio's comment and post two reasons why I think this is such a great point.' Outside of webinars, students should be encouraged to have their images or avatars on the VLE, and should be encouraged to personalise their home pages, so that they feel this is their environment and not just a place they are occasionally asked to enter.

In asking our students to engage with learning in this way, it is really important that we clearly outline our expectations of online learning – giving super-clear instructions. In the face-to-face classroom, we are able to intervene when we see that students are struggling or need clarification on a point. It is harder to intervene when teaching online, as activities are often set up so that students can do things in their own time. In this way, the structure of online teaching and learning activities needs to be as transparent as possible with clear signposting. For each activity we need to foreground our support with instructions such as: this is what I would like you to do > this is how you might do it > this is where you can find out more information > these are the tools you can use to complete the task > this is where you can post your finished task > this is where you can review and comment on the work of fellow students.

Online teaching should be underpinned by the principles, ideas, structures and perspectives that are discussed throughout this book. We don't need to panic just because the modality has changed. Online learning is more than just trying to remember fact and figures; therefore, online teaching should be about the guided development of a series of activities – with a clear beginning, middle and end, and a clear sense of challenge and reward. This is not to say that there is only one model of online teaching, but, whether we are teaching online or face-to-face, the endoskeletal approach to teaching means that we have both structure and flexibility.

THREE MODELS OF TEACHING

There are many different ways to teach and learn and these should, of course, relate to how each individual sees their role, their students' needs and expectations, and institutional or departmental norms. Models of teaching may even relate to how much control we have over the physical environment and how much influence we have over setting the criteria for success. Decisions about teaching have to be made and remade constantly in response to changing situations and students' needs, so we shouldn't feel that we need to choose the 'best' model and stick with it. As with everything in higher education, the answer always involves the teacher making an informed decision about what is best, when and why.

The three teaching models described on the following pages facilitate a structured approach to learning. Most teaching in higher education involves a variation on the themes of 'define', 'do' and 'review'. Sometimes the definitions are presented by the teacher, sometimes they are developed by the students, sometimes they emerge from the teaching environment itself and sometimes students are asked to learn definitions ahead of class through independent enquiry. The 'do' stage of learning is my favourite because the students are asked to apply and make sense out of what they have learned – undertaking tasks to help them interpret what has been defined. Finally, students (sometimes with their teachers and sometimes with their peers) should get a chance to interrogate their learning and review how it fits into their existing framework of understanding. However, the themes of define, do and review don't necessarily have to happen in that order, and creative teachers will find ways to mix them up.

The three models outlined in this section work alongside the concept of the three-part seminar and allow for the stages of define, do and review. While there are many teaching models, these are the most common approaches:

1   Whole-class teaching – all students learning the same thing at the same time.

2   Resource-based teaching – all students learning the same thing at different times.

3   Self-directed learning – all students learning different things at different times.

What is the best model (or the best blend) for your specific learning situation?

WHOLE-CLASS TEACHING

There are two main versions of whole-class teaching: the first, *leading from the front*, uses a deductive pedagogy, whereas the second, *directing from the rear*, uses an inductive pedagogy.

LEADING FROM THE FRONT

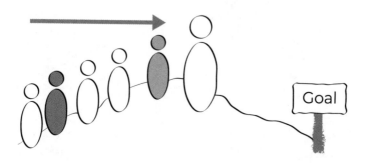

Leading from the front involves using a clear system of demonstration and definition. Key concepts are explained or illustrated – students are shown the 'right' way to do something and then asked to follow this process in their own learning. Under this deductive model, the whole class has the same expected outcome – and the teacher, who knows what the end point looks like, provides them with the necessary skills in order for them to be successful. Most teaching in higher education looks a bit like this: the students are given a system and then asked to repeat that system. The trouble is that there isn't always much room for initiative or autonomy, which can frustrate some individuals. And if we are seeking to develop student agency, then this model doesn't offer a great deal of scope for originality or personal preference either. Like most teaching models, the secret is not to rely on a single format but to use the appropriate model at the appropriate time.

DIRECTING FROM THE REAR

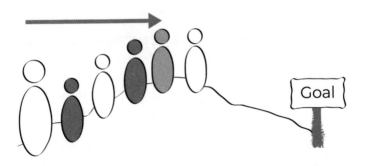

As with leading from the front, all the students are expected to reach the same goal with directing from the rear. The difference is that the teaching does not start with demonstration; it starts by setting the parameters of success. Under this model, the teacher sets out what success will look like, perhaps in terms of an assessment the students will undertake. These learning outcomes will be clearly shared and all the students will know what is expected of them. This inductive approach offers scope for some level of individuality because the students can decide what route they think will work for them. The focus is not only on following instructions and doing things in the usual ways, but also on students solving their own problems and finding their own path to success. Throughout this process the teacher has a shepherding role – keeping an overview and nudging the students back on track when they stray too far. This is often best done through questioning individuals – for example, 'Why did you decide to do X?' or 'What do you think an alternative method might be?'

RESOURCE-BASED TEACHING

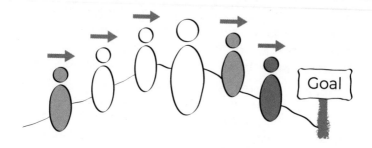

The focus of resource-based teaching is on enabling students to reach a common goal. In most cases this is an assessment of some kind. However, the learning does not happen as one group unit; instead, each student learns at their own pace and takes an individual approach to reaching the final goal. A good example of this would be the development of a portfolio of work. By the end of the year, all of the students will have a solid portfolio of work, but the various artefacts will vary according to individual choices. For example, one student might demonstrate their understanding of thermodynamics by creating a leaflet, another might do a literature review and a third might create a conference presentation. In all three cases, the artefact itself is less important than the student being able to demonstrate their level of understanding or competence.

Many people teaching in higher education have trouble with resource-based teaching, but I believe this is usually because they have misunderstood the nature of assessment. Assessment generally has two aspects: the tool being used (exam, assignment, presentation, etc.) and the content being assessed. The former is simply the means of evaluating the latter. It is the level of a student's understanding that we need to focus on, not the mechanism by which we measure it.

Resource-based teaching moves away from the idea that all students need to be doing the same thing at the same time, and also away from the idea that all students need to be assessed using the same tools. Instead, we create a model that starts by setting out the skills, knowledge and understanding we are aiming to develop, then we establish a means of measuring those abilities, and finally we permit flexibility in how aptitude is demonstrated. Likewise, it is possible that the timescale is such that each student can develop different aspects of their learning at different times. This approach can also be applied to group work where a bunch of students work as an individual learning unit. Under this model, our job is not to teach per se, but to guide and offer support as and when required – we might imagine an artist moving around a studio suggesting individualised input on each person's work.

Resource-based teaching is most frequently misunderstood when a specific field of study is identified with a specific form of assessment – a misconception which is often reinforced by signature pedagogies. It is true that fewer assessment options are available with certain subjects, but it is always worth exploring other ways for students to show their learning. Mathematics sometimes gets a bad reputation as a field where things are black or white, right or wrong, but in fact it has a great history of embracing multiple means for showing the same outcome. In maths there is often a process (a sum) and an outcome (an answer). The answer might be universal but the way that students achieve that answer allows for many different approaches; as long as the processes are rigorous and coherent they should be regarded as equally legitimate. If a maths teacher insists that their students use only one method in order to find the answer, then they need a strong rationale for doing so; if not, the students should be permitted at least some control over how they work. The focus here is not on giving instructions, but asking probing questions and pushing students to be reflective examiners of their own learning and learning outcomes.

SELF-DIRECTED LEARNING

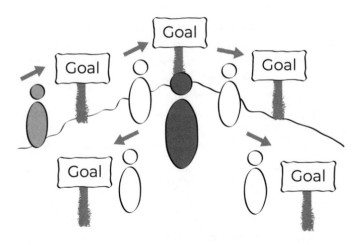

Self-directed learning is similar to resource-based teaching in that students are working at their own pace; the difference is that each student has their own criteria for success and their own timeline. The most common version of self-directed learning in higher education is where students are working on dissertations or theses. The role of the teacher is not to give instruction but to be a supportive facilitator or guide. In post-graduate study, we might find ourselves working with a handful of students who are each at different stages of their research process. Some will finish soon and some may be years off. Each person needs something specific from us. The secret here is not to offer too much help. This type of learning is about autonomy, and it is hard for a student to develop autonomy when we show or tell them what to do. Instead, what our students need is guidance by way of questions, hints, tips and praise.

COMMUNICATION

When we consider types of teaching, we should also consider how we are perceived by our students. Using different pedagogies allows us to add variety and enables us to base our teaching decisions on what we feel is the best blend at any given moment. These diverse models of delivery and methods of meeting learning outcomes are also underpinned by the way in which we communicate with our students. If we choose to teach through a lecture (a very tricky skill to get right), then we need to consider how we use our voice as much as the words we actually use. Likewise, if we are teaching a group of 12 students in a seminar room and they are all engaged in small group work, we need to consider how we project our voice so that we can bring activities to a close and draw out key learning.

Since this section is about the structure of teaching in higher education, it is worth reflecting on how we manage our personal interactions in the learning environment. Communication is not just something that happens – it needs to be thought through and organised. What follows are some basic pointers on structuring our communication. I have tried to make these as generic as possible: some will come easily to you and others might seem 'fake', but do try to give them a go. I have broken down the hints into four sections: voice, gesture, eye contact and composition. Try to consider these points in relation to the teaching models discussed thus far, because the range of voice, gesture, eye contact and composition will change depending on whether you are teaching using whole-class, resource-based or self-directed learning.

VOICE

Aim to use variety in your voice. If you speak in the same monotone for an entire class then someone will fall asleep. Conversely, if you present everything as being super-exciting then how will your students know what really matters? Here are some adjustments you can make:

- Change the volume from forceful to soft to emphasise the significance of a topic.

- Change the speed and tempo to show excitement, awe and wonder.

- Pause to breathe to give dramatic emphasis and room for the students to think.

Also think about how you can project your voice. It is really frustrating when someone from the back of the room yells out, 'I can't hear you!' – so, when you speak, aim your voice at the back wall. You can improve this by looking at the wall occasionally and imagining your voice travelling there.

Avoid verbal tics such as 'um', 'ah', 'OK' and so on. Most of us have these habits and they are especially obvious when we are mentally looking for the right word or phrase. You can learn to restructure your speech so you replace verbal tics with silence. Instead of saying it out loud, try saying 'um' in your head by closing your mouth when you are mentally searching for your next statement. This will create a very short silence (which might seem like ages to you but will in fact be only one or two seconds) during which your students will get a chance to think – and see you thinking too. In this way, a clumsy sounding 'err' can become a thoughtful space in time.

Once you have successfully replaced verbal tics with short pauses, you can start to make these pauses work for you – using them for emphasis and to highlight when students should be reflecting on a point. This technique works well in lectures where lots of information is shared in a short period of time and it can be beneficial to have a short pause. It is also useful in small seminar groups and in lab work or fieldwork, where you may want the class to stop an activity in order to refocus them on a wider point. For example, you might halt group activities and say, '[pause] Let's stop there for a moment and have a look at some examples. [pause] Gather round this table so we can [pause] focus on how our projects link to the [pause] theories we looked at earlier.'

GESTURE

The way you present your physical being, the way you move around and the way you gesticulate should be controlled and purposeful. Think about the messages you wish to convey in your body language and use gesture to add emphasis to specific points. Here are some simple guidelines:

● Don't stand in one place. Move around but avoid pacing.

● When a student is speaking try not to walk towards them; instead, take half a step back.

- Move your hands and arms when you speak to enhance your points.

- Avoid distracting the learners by jiggling change in your pocket, clicking a pen, waving a pointer, constant throat-clearing, swaying around and so on.

- Stand when you wish to command attention and sit when you want to leave the limelight.

- Avoid using laser pointers – half the class can't see the red dot as it's too small and moves too fast. Also, they are just not cool!

When considering your body language and gestures, try to focus on how they will be perceived by students. For example, standing too close to an individual can make them feel uncomfortable and may impact on their learning, and lurking or fidgeting around in the background during group work can distract the students and reduce their interactions with peers. Finally, try to correlate the size of your gestures with the size of the room. Large lecture theatres need bigger sweeps of the arm and whole-body movements, while smaller venues might be better suited to movements of the hands or fingers.

EYE CONTACT

Eye contact is a valuable tool that reinforces human connection. It is a good way of conveying a message of inclusivity and communicating that you are interested in your students. It can also quickly send the message that you are looking for engagement from them. These pointers should help to form that link:

- Look at the students rather than your PowerPoint.

- Scan the group and glance at everyone, not just the supportive faces.

- When making eye contact, mentally show acknowledgement to the person (e.g. think nice thoughts – they will appear as micro-gestures on your face).

- In large groups, it can be hard to form eye contact with every student, so try to scan larger zones of the room.

- Don't speak while the students are reading – they can only do one thing at a time.

- Don't speak when you are writing on the board. Like your students, you can only do one thing at a time. You will either say something wrong or spell something wrong.

- When answering a question, look at the entire group, not just the questioner. End by looking at the questioner for a sign that the answer was sufficient.

Eye contact often works in conjunction with facial expressions, so try not to be so focused on establishing eye contact with the students that you forget to smile. Eye contact without a smile can be creepy! Eye contact should not be just one way – that is, from teacher to student. All students should be able to make eye contact with you (if they so choose) to hint that they understand, that they have a question or that they are struggling with a concept. This means that you should occupy a space in the teaching environment that enables the students to easily catch your eye, so don't wander up to the back of the lecture hall or seminar room because the students at the front will find it hard to get your attention.

COMPOSITION

By reflecting on the component parts of your teaching, you can keep a check on the volume of information you are communicating, as well as maintaining a balance between the activity undertaken by yourself and your students. Here are a few easy wins:

- Share the structure of the class/lecture/seminar with the students.

- Ask frequent questions.

- Build in reviews.

- Try to minimise your own talking time.

- Don't use lengthy notes – free yourself from notes as much as possible so that you can focus on organising learning activities rather than teacher-talk.

As well as reflecting on how you balance the various components of your teaching session, you should also aim to think about how you use them. For example, examples and anecdotes have different functions in the learning environment and elicit different types of response. Examples should be used to clarify a point and show how it might work in 'real life', so they need to be well-thought-through and transferable. Examples can be generic or specific. Generic examples are broad statements that support your point – for instance, you might be teaching a class on musical notation and state that tempo is a standard annotation that is used in many music scores. You might also give the specific example of how the notation for the fingered bass is different from the notation on the score for percussion. In both instances there is some transferable knowledge. In the first case, students can look for typical annotation that exists across many music scores, and in the second they can explore why some instruments might need a specific type of notation. An example can often be followed up by a request for the students to think of another similar illustration. This not only places an emphasis on student activity but also helps you to check their learning.

In contrast, anecdotes tend to emerge from personal experience and are less likely to be transferable, although they often highlight the inherent problems of certain ideas. You are unlikely to ask the students if they have a similar anecdote, but you can ask them what they think you learned from your experience and what they have learned from hearing about it. In this way, we can see compositional links between one phase of the session (the example/anecdote) and the next phase (the student inter-rogation of the example/anecdote).

Last, but not least, while concentrating on your voice, gesture, eye contact and composition – aim to be natural!

THREE CHALLENGES

1 **Try to think about learning a structured series of activities.** Don't plan what you are going to teach; plan what your students are going to learn. Then design a series of activities that will help them to develop and demonstrate that learning. Teaching isn't about the delivery of long monologues. It's about the facilitation of a series of learning events. Learning can be chaotic, disjointed and disorganised (and that's OK), but, in order to balance this, teaching must be structured and purposeful. The best learning doesn't need to be over-planned but the worst learning is usually under-planned. Always share the structure of a session with the students – for example, write a list of

bullet points on the board at the start of the session to highlight the various phases you will be focusing on. You should also try to structure how you want the students to respond. For instance, when introducing a major assignment or project, don't ask vaguely if there are 'Any questions?' Instead, ask the students to work in threes to identify what success will look like (four minutes), any barriers to success (three minutes) and then review as a whole class (eight minutes). When planning various phases into your session, you could even consider using a pre-existing structure such as a dissertation or thesis. Each phase might have a heading, such as background, literature, data, theory and case study. Select the right mix of phases, add an introduction and conclusion and, hey presto, you have a structure!

2 **Try to add structure to group work.** High-quality higher education is not reliant on what we do but what we ask the students to do. If we want our students to be engaged, then we had better design educational activities that are worth engaging with. Group work can offer real scope for engagement and interaction but it needs to be well thought-through. Group work is great, but it can tend towards compromise and capitulation to the loudest voices. Instead of using group work to answer questions, try using it to generate lists of different perspectives – brainstorming possibilities rather than presenting absolute answers.

The make-up of a group can be a key factor in its success or failure, so we need to examine the rationale behind how we configure our groups and the challenges we set them. Size really does matter. Groups of more than four members tend to be ineffective as they break up into sub-groups, so three is the perfect number. (Make sure you have a good pedagogical reason if and when you work with larger groups – and it's best to pick the group members yourself!) As well as keeping groups small, make sure you give them clear instructions, share the success criteria and keep timeframes short. To avoid dominant students taking over, adopt a *Lord of the Flies* conch approach by using two flip-chart marker pens: no one can speak unless they are holding a pen. Whoever is holding the red marker can offer suggestions and whoever is holding the blue marker can offer alternatives. Once you have set the rules of engagement for group work, it is important to take a step back and let groups do their own learning for (at least) the first five minutes. One of the hardest things in teaching is letting the students learn for themselves.

3 **Try to plan sessions with a clear beginning, middle and end.** The first thing students should hear coming out of your mouth should not be an instruction, learning outcome or anecdote. It should be a friendly greeting. It sets the tone and shows the students that this will be a human experience. Setting the tone should only take a minute; the rest of the introduction should be taken up with explaining to students what they will be focusing on and what will be learned. Too many colleagues assume that their students already know what the topic is and so just get right down to the nitty-gritty. We shouldn't assume that all students have checked the schedule before arriving. During this introductory phase, try not to say, 'Today I'd like to talk about X' but instead, say, 'Today I'd like you to think about X.'

The middle phase of the session should include a series of learning tasks. Generally, each task should not take up more than 20% of the entire class time before a change of focus is introduced. Halfway through a class, ask the students to write down three questions they would like answered before they finish (at the end you can ask them to rewrite their initial questions with improved or more focused versions). Plan for the key phase of your teaching to take place two-thirds of the way through.

Ending a class well is an art form, so make sure you plan a clear structured conclusion. Don't just suddenly stop because you have run out of time, and never finish class late. Three minutes before you are due to stop, the students will be mentally and physically packing up. No one learns during the overrun period, so it's better to stop five minutes early and support the students to reflect on what they have learned. At the end of class, ask them to write down the answers to three simple questions: (1) What did I learn? (2) Why should I care? and (3) How will I apply this understanding? These quick student reflections are not intended to be a way for the teacher to assess the learning that has occurred; rather, the focus should be on encouraging students to be thoughtful in their learning and to mentally log their own understanding and progress.

LITTLE NUGGETS OF WISDOM

STRUCTURE

- Teaching is the impossible art of finding the right balance.

- Classes tend to have three steps: define, do and review. Imagine how much more engaging learning could be if the 'do' phase came first!

- Feedback should also be in three parts: this is your grade, here's why you got it and here are three clear ways to improve.

- Halfway through student feedback on their group task is not a teachable moment. Wait until everyone has fed back and then return to the key points raised.

- A top teaching skill is the ability to know when to stop explaining things to bored students and let them get on with doing the learning.

TIMING

- Teachers who tell their students that they are 'aware of the time' are really saying that the session is going to overrun.

- As a rough guide when giving a lecture, aim to have a five-second break every five minutes. Students need thinking space – and you do too.

- Don't write a script for your class. Instead, write down ten bullet points – nine points you wish to cover and one to tell you to slow down.

- Imagine that the total number of words in any class is finite. If you use up more than your share with teacher-talk, then you won't leave much time for student debate, discussion and interaction.

- You may have planned for 10 minutes of feedback but you know it will take longer!

PITCH

- Learning should be slightly out of reach so the students have to make an effort. The instant they grasp one concept, move the goal further away.

- Try to pitch the level of your teaching just above where you think the middle ground is, and then use examples to clarify and questions to extend their thinking.

- Personalised learning doesn't mean teaching everyone individually; it means treating everyone as an individual.

- Students benefit from targets but they have to believe in the target first, so try getting them to set their own goals based on honest reflection.

- It might not be that your question is too hard – it might be too long! Tricky questions need to be short and sweet.

CHAPTER 3

THE FLOW OF INFORMATION

I have been observing teaching for over 20 years in one way or another. During this time I have drawn maps of the teaching environment. This began as a way of charting which student was sitting in which chair, but I gradually started to use it as a tool for recording information, interactions and activity. As an observer, I draw maps during the observation process, but I also create them after my own teaching sessions as I reflect on the relative success or failure of my practice.

For me, mapping works best at the whole-class level – where the teaching involves leading a discussion or running a question-and-answer session. This form of teaching can be mentally draining and physically exhausting as we are trying to steer the group through a series of deliberations and towards a critical understanding of the subject matter. Therefore, mapping the learning environment allows me to measure levels of engagement at the whole-class level by noting how active each individual student was and examining how their peers responded. Mapping is not about whether an individual understands a given topic; rather, it is about how students share information with their peers and work together to interrogate ideas. Helping students to be active is a key teaching skill, and mapping the learning environment helps us to notice not just activity but also interactivity.

Over time, some of my maps have become rather elaborate as I have developed codes, symbols and ciphers as a way of representing many of the types of activity that take place in a typical teaching session, but here I am going to focus on maps that relate to information flow. It is extremely valuable to reflect on a session you have taught and map the teaching–learning dynamic. It is often easier to notice this when observing others, so you might start with that and then move into a more reflective phase.

TEACHING THROUGH MODELLING

The classroom or seminar room is only one of the areas where teaching happens in higher education: teaching also happens in lecture halls, computer labs, science labs and during fieldwork. A combination of these teaching formats also exists online. The principle of mapping the flow of information remains the same in all these settings – we just need to be a bit more creative. The first example below illustrates a seminar room but the same movement of information can easily be applied to a lab environment or lecture hall.

I have drawn the following map all too often:

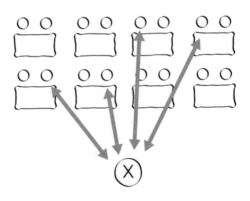

It shows information flowing back and forth from the teacher to an individual student. A common instance of this involves the teacher asking a question, getting an answer and then asking another question. Some students will volunteer an answer, some will be nominated but most will stay quiet. In this example, the information moves from the teacher to the student body. Each piece of shared information is then experienced and interpreted by the students at an individual level. The teaching here is about controlling the pace and direction of the session, but there is no information flowing from student to student. In a lecture format this information flow is likely to remain constant, but in labs and seminars it would (hopefully) represent just one phase of the session. The trouble with a model where the flow of information is from teacher to learner is that, even when they have their own questions, the students start to feel that their job is to supply the answers that are in the teacher's head.

It is usual for seminars and lab sessions to start with this type of teaching, but there is a danger if this goes on for too long: after a while, the students learn that their role is to listen and take notes. The teacher may expect their students to ask questions, but the more they talk, the fewer questions they receive. This is one of the reasons why, after 15 minutes of teacher-talk, when asked if there are 'Any questions?' very few students say anything. At this point some teachers get frustrated and wonder why their students aren't engaging. The answer is because they have modelled a system in which the students are not expected to engage, and then they have suddenly changed the dynamic and expected them to instantly flip from passive to active learners.

MATCHING YOUR PEDAGOGY TO THE ENVIRONMENT

In my second map, the layout of the desks may have changed but the flow of information is still from the teacher to the students:

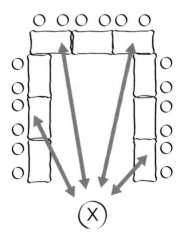

One of the features of horseshoe layouts is the increased likelihood of discussion through face-to-face interaction, but this only occurs if the adopted pedagogy enables it. Moving the furniture is a great idea (if practicable in your setting) as it enables new interactions to take place, but this must be reinforced through modelled practice. Simple actions like asking the students to turn to their neighbour and create a list of the key points covered so far demonstrates to them that they are expected to reflect and engage with each other. But this is only the starting point – we also need to model a system of analysis by showing students different approaches to picking an idea apart in an academic and analytical manner.

GETTING STUDENTS INTERACTIVE WITH INFORMATION

The next map is one of my favourites and shows how information moves around the room, is examined by various members of the group and then there is further deliberation on the points raised:

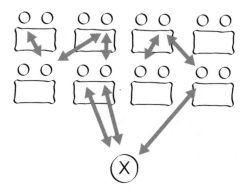

The focus here should be on creating an environment in which information flows from student to student and ideas are developed and critically debated. The role of the teacher is to keep the discussion going by asking open questions that encourage debate. Once the first student has offered an answer, we should seek supporting or opposing positions, perhaps encouraging the students to argue from a theoretical or philosophical perspective. After a while, the students no longer need to be prompted – they become accustomed to being part of a critical discussion and expect to be involved. In practice, we might start by sharing an insightful quotation, a new research article or a devil's advocate-type suggestion. The job of this starter artefact is to elicit comment. Once shared with the group, we are looking for two quick reactions. Other students are then asked to react to their peers' thoughts – building on points they agree with and offering alternative perspectives where they differ. After bouncing the idea around the room for three or four minutes, each student is then asked to write a 99-word summary of their thinking. This whole activity may have taken about nine minutes and would have involved two important academic skills – critical thinking and the data synthesis.

This interactive flow of information can also happen in a VLE. Too often, students are expected to comment on discussion boards but there is little scaffolding to support this. This means that a few students will regularly comment, a few more will comment infrequently and some will be virtually silent (pun intended). Instead of just creating an online discussion forum and hoping the students will say interesting things, we can create a staged structure (similar to the one described above) where the students are given an initial learning artefact and asked to post their 20-word first impressions on the message board. Once they have done so, they are each asked to add some constructive comments on two of their peers' posts. Finally, the students are asked to create a table of responses, drawing on the points raised and the positive critiques offered. In this table, the students should try to group various responses into themes. I am not suggesting that this is a perfect task – my aim is that you adapt it and make it your own – but it does provide a template where the flow of information is scaffolded and expected.

PAIRED DISCUSSION

This map shows the very least amount of student activity that I expect in a teaching/learning session:

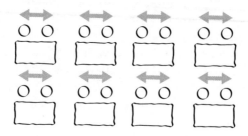

In this instance, the students work in pairs to discuss, analyse or examine a topic, question or artefact. The information flows from student to student and the role of the teacher is to facilitate feedback and organise the responses the pairs give into a more general answer. The pairs don't even need to feed back to the whole class – they can be partnered with other pairs and share their thoughts in small groups.

This type of paired discussion needs to be task-focused and time-focused. If students are given the rather vague task of 'talking it over with their neighbour for five or ten minutes', they are likely to feel frustrated by the lack of support. It is better to be very clear about what you want them to do – for example, create a list of three reasons why X won't work, link back to two topics already covered in this module, write a user guide, create a flow chart and so on – and then give them a short time to complete it.

The problem with saying that a task should take 'five or ten minutes' is that you are communicating that you don't know how long the task should take, which doesn't give a very good impression. Instead, try telling the students that they have seven minutes. A precise number tends to get their attention because it sounds like a very specific amount of time and that you have thought about it carefully. Give the students a two-minute warning and then a final countdown from five to one. Then ask them to stop. If you think the task will take longer than seven minutes, try to split it into sections. In this way, they do part one during the first seven minutes, pause and feed back their initial findings, and then move on to part two of the task. If you think the students will need a long period of time to complete the task, then you might wish to rethink your planning. As a rough rule of thumb, no single student task should take up more than one third of the class time (and there should be more than one task in each session).

MAPPING THE LEARNING ENVIRONMENT

Mapping the way that information flows in the teaching environment gives us an overview of who is actually doing the work and enables us to see if a class is more teacher centred or student centred. Admittedly, mapping is quite a blunt tool and should always be used in conjunction with more thoughtful reflective practice, but I find it to be a really useful way of getting an overview of how active or passive the student group has been. My more nuanced maps also show the level of participation of individual students, the student who asked the first question (and when this occurred), the position of the teacher at various phases of the session and whether the teacher was mainly looking at the class or looking at the board. There are likely to be lots of variations on this technique and my general model could be personalised to suit individual tastes, but I recommend this to others as a way of examining aspects of their practice. Drawing these maps doesn't take much time or talent but the results can be a purposeful catalyst for development. The principle is most clearly evident in face-to-face seminars and lectures, but there is also scope to consider this in small group tutorials and even one-to-one sessions.

Because of the implied hierarchical model of higher education, many students do not feel comfortable being too challenging in environments where they perceive themselves to be vulnerable. During a one-to-one tutorial these students might become passive, which can sometimes lead to awkward silences. These silences are often filled by teacher-talk, where we explain ideas or point out areas where they could develop their learning. The teacher often assumes a de facto power role and can easily be perceived as the source of all wisdom. If we were to map this information flow over a number of sessions, it would reveal that the flow of information is mainly from (active) teacher to (passive) student – we talk and our student listens. This situation is not satisfactory for either party. We want our students to talk so that we can gauge their level of understanding and so that they can feel empowered.

In order to create a better flow of information in a tutorial-type environment, we may wish to do two things. This first one is tricky: be prepared to leave long awkward silences! Generally, if you wait long enough the student will talk. I recommend counting to 15 in your head after you ask a question in a small group or individual tutorial situation. If you have no response after 15 seconds, ask a simple follow-up question such as, 'What do you think?' and then wait for around seven seconds. This can feel very uncomfortable, but you are demonstrating that there is a space for student input.

The second option is less awkward and involves creating a clear working framework and making this explicit to the student. The nature of tutorials means that planning can sometimes be overlooked and arrangements rather loose. While teachers tend to (and should) structure their classroom-based teaching, we are likely to see tutorials as a more discursive environment (an academic chat) where we don't need to be so rigid in our planning. However, I would suggest that tutorials are always run using the same format and that both parties are fully aware of the elements of that format.

This structure is shared with the student(s) at the start of each session, during which we outline the various topics we will be discussing and who should take the lead on each phase. This might mean that the tutorial starts with a student-led update on what they have done since last time or what they have read that will help their studies. We might then ask some brief closed questions. These are useful at this stage as closed questions are usually easily answered and also reinforce the back and forth of information that we wish to create. Examples of closed questions might include: 'Did you attend Professor Brown's lecture?', 'Did you read that article I sent you?', 'When is the deadline?' or 'Have you read through the course learning outcomes?' These questions are a little pushy, because they suggest to the student that you expect them to engage with these activities, but they are also straightforward and indicate that you want them to talk. Once a dialogue has been established, we can start asking more open and probing questions: 'How will you relate the theory covered last week to your assignment?' or 'Why did you decide to choose option 1?'

Whether we are teaching in a large lecture hall or working one-to-one with students on their academic work, there is a flow of information. If we map this flow (I suggest that you do this on paper initially but it may evolve into a mental process later on), then we can start to see the relationship between what we planned to do and what actually happened. In this way, we can make changes that will help to create a learning environment in which students are not just expected to engage, but are given the space and the framework to do so.

Too often, teaching in higher education starts with thinking about the facts to be learned and the processes for checking this learning. Offering our students a framework for developing their critical thinking means that any subsequent assessment will be focused on evaluating not just what they have learned but also the utility of that information, allowing us to explore two important questions, 'What has been learned?' and 'What can we do with this new learning?' The first of these questions is focused on knowledge, while the second seeks to explore a student's level of understanding. Once we encourage information to flow in a more dynamic manner – from teacher to student, from student to student, and from student to teacher – we start to move away from the idea that the learning environment is a place where information is simply passed from one person to another and we start to see it as a place where information is scrutinised by all.

ASSESSMENT ISN'T JUST ABOUT THE END POINT

There are three elements to gaining a UK motorcycle licence. In the first stage you must obtain a provisional licence and complete a compulsory basic training (CBT) certificate to ride on public roads. You can then ride, displaying L plates, for up to two years on a motorbike with an engine below 125cc. Before the two years are up, you must complete a theory test and a practical test. First, the CBT is assessed by an experienced instructor on a track off the public highway. The instructor judges whether you are competent to handle a motorbike based on a number of set tasks and criteria. Next, the theory test takes place in a computer suite where you are asked for your responses to a number of questions and assessed for your reaction time in a series of potentially dangerous scenarios. The final test takes place on the road – an examiner follows you on their motorbike and speaks to you through a headset as you ride through traffic. The examiner appraises your ability to perform certain manoeuvres and marks you down for each error you make. Getting a licence involves three forms of summative assessment, but in actual fact there is a lot more assessment going on.

From the moment I first sat on a motorbike I was self-assessing: was I really going to do this? Could I handle the complicated gear changes? Would I crash? I was also self-assessing throughout the period I was learning. I knew that I was good at finding my position on the road but my gear selection was poor. I could negotiate roundabouts but I found it difficult to turn at slow speed. When I found myself in motorbike shops buying helmets, gloves and waterproofs, I felt like a fake. I was surrounded by people I assumed to be 'real' bikers; they were cool and knew the lingo, but I was an outsider pretending I knew what I was doing. Even when I had gained my licence, I was not convinced that I was legitimate. My reflections told me that I was not yet the finished article and that I needed more time on the road to truly feel I had made it. But after many years on the road, I am still learning and still asking myself questions.

THE PROCESS–PRODUCT MODEL OF ASSESSMENT

For many, assessment is conceptualised as an end point: we learn X and then we are tested on X. But my motorbike example suggests that to simply focus on the assessment of the product is rather naive. There is also much to be gained from assessing the process. Whether we are acquiring a physical skill or trying to understand conceptual knowledge, there is a process of learning taking place, and throughout the learning event the learner is involved in reflective self-assessment. Assessment isn't something that only comes at the end of a period of learning; instructors, lecturers and supervisors also assess their students as they develop their learning. My CBT instructors didn't just judge my capacity at the end of the course. They were assessing me constantly and refining their teaching based on their evaluation of my needs. Research supervisors do the same thing: draft chapters and tutorial discussions are where the processes of research are assessed. No thesis is ever assessed only once it is complete.

The process–product model of assessment can help us to see the breadth of assessment that is taking place throughout the learning experience, and it is very hard to have one without the other. An end-point assessment is not really an end. Once a student has passed a course or gained a qualification, they don't suddenly claim to be an expert and nor do they purge themselves of this 'completed' knowledge in order to make way for new learning. Product assessment simply moves the learner on to the next stage of their learning, where they will become involved in another process assessment. From this perspective, assessment is constant but its form changes.

I have been involved in education my whole life – as a student and a teacher. But I have not yet actually 'completed' any learning because every time I take an exam, gain a qualification or write a paper, I move on to the next phase, and then the next phase, and then the next. In this way, I will never *learn* anything but I will always be *learning*. Understanding the breadth of assessment is not simply a matter of knowing about the many ways that the product of learning can be assessed; it is also about understanding the many ways that the *process* of learning can be assessed.

DO WE REALLY NEED ASSESSMENT?

Assessment is everywhere. From written essays to group projects. From multiple choice questions to reflective accounts. From summative to formative. From January to December. From this day on, now and forever more. There is assessment *of* learning, assessment *for* learning, assessment *in* learning and assessment *as* learning. Individuals fill their curriculum vitae with qualifications and add pre-nominal titles and post-nominal letters to their names. Organisations are inspected and append markers of compliance to their letterheads. And the entire system is checked against the global standards of bodies such as the International Organization for Standardization, the Occupational Health and Safety Assessment Series and the World Health Organization. Like grocers' apostrophes, once you become aware of assessment you start seeing it everywhere, all the time, non-stop, 24/7. So, do we really need all of this assessment?

Students are assessed formatively and summatively throughout their time in higher education, but are we assessing or are we over-assessing? Perhaps the time is right for an assessment cull. If so, one place to start would be exams. Not only do exams take up a lot of time, effort and logistical shenanigans, but they do not always achieve their stated intentions. Exams do not do what many people think they do. A reduction in the volume of assessment would involve chopping out the deadwood of examinations and replacing it with time and space for educational growth. Exams are part of the presumed system of educational assessment, but do we really need them or are they just the legacy of a signature pedagogy of education?

When we consider the process–product debate, we discover that exams are quite poor tools for assessing critical thinking and the synthesis of knowledge. They are terrific at assessing recall, but is that what higher education learning is really about? The issue might be that when we ask colleagues how students will be assessed, the question and the answer both focus on the format of the assessment and therefore on the tools used: examinations, lab practicals, portfolios and so on.

It is important to remember what it is we are actually assessing – that is, knowledge, skills and understanding. The assumption is that exams 'check' learning but they do so only in a very narrow way. Exams are useful for testing the teaching–learning dynamic by asking questions that expose current levels of knowledge, but in order to give balance to content knowledge, we also need to explore the impact of this knowledge on the overall development of the student and the evolution of their conceptual thinking. If we default to assuming that end-point assessments like exams are the 'true' measure of learning, then there is a danger that we lose focus on the significance of the application of learning.

As well as reflecting on the justification for exams, we also need to take time out to think about the way that examinations are actually conducted – and whether there is anything to be learned from this. If one of the jobs of higher education is to prepare students for employment, then we might argue that exams aren't much use after the event and that they really only exist in their own little bubble. Exams pretend that the real world does not exist and force students into draughty halls with only a few pens at their disposal. They sit in silent rows for hours on end in an effort to recall information that is on their smartphones and in their notes at home. The students have access to the information, but the exam denies them that access!

Exams also force examiners to make some weird choices. Every year, they create papers with 'new' questions which are kept locked away until the day of the exam. But thousands of previous exam papers exist and are stored in libraries across the country for students to peruse during the revision period. Examiners find themselves tasked with creating fresh sets of questions that test for the same things the old questions tested for but with a slight change in emphasis. The 'newness' of these new papers is therefore debatable. Exam papers are treated like precious jewels before the exam, and then immediately afterwards they become worthless and are cast aside.

In short, there are at least three points that need to be considered with regard to exams: whether exams are the right tools to check for student learning, whether learning the skills of sitting an exam is useful in the longer term, and whether all the effort required to create, invigilate and mark exams is worth it. The argument against exams has become stronger over time as higher education institutions recognise their limitations. This has led to an increase in coursework, presentations, practicals and other forms of assessment. But it is worth applying the same argument to all forms of assessment: are they are fit for purpose and truly suited to accessing the deeper levels of understanding that we hope to inspire in our students? Assessment is useful when it is considered in its broadest form – as an evaluation of process and product – but if we spend too much time focused on trying to assess the end point of learning, then we soon find that the justification for many modes of assessment is not as strong as we might assume it to be.

A GREATER FOCUS ON UNDERSTANDING

There are only really two questions in education: 'What?' and 'So what?' The former tests for knowledge and the latter tests for understanding. In developing closed-book examinations, the system has privileged the retrieval of knowledge over the application of knowledge. A more realistic assessment process would allow students full access to notes, books, tablets, laptops, the internet, peers, professors, aunts, uncles and grandparents. Instead of squirming away in the fakery of the exam hall, assessments would be set up in the full knowledge that students have access to all available facts, figures and formulae. In shifting the emphasis from testing for knowledge to testing for understanding, the focus would move from 'What?' to 'So what?' as students would have to use their talents to craft persuasive arguments, juggle opposing positions in the literature, work within academic traditions and meet set deadlines.

When we conceptualise assessment as a simple test of what a student can remember, our pedagogy is likely to bend to accommodate this conceptualisation. If we know that students will be assessed on X, Y and Z, then we are likely to teach X, Y and Z. The danger of this model is that it narrows the curriculum and we start to teach for the test rather than teaching for learning. We live in a credential age, in which gaining qualifications opens up job opportunities. As a result, students have learned to be strategic – to focus on what will be assessed and what will lead to the best outcomes for them. This is no one's fault: it is simply a product of neoliberalism, where knowledge has become a commodity. By asking questions such as, 'Will this be in the assignment?', the subtext is that, if a piece of learning is not going to be assessed, then it might not be worthwhile learning it in the first place. Conversely, if we consider learning to be a wider and more empowering process, then the answer to this question is, 'It might not be in the assignment, but knowing it will probably make your assignment better overall.'

Another issue with product-focused assessment is that rote learning is actually quite a good way of getting students to remember things. (I know I shouldn't admit this, but it's true.) The downside is that while rote learning improves knowledge retention, it does not support knowledge application. I can still remember a poem by Robert Burns from when I had to recite it aged 9, but I don't really know what the poem is about. Focusing on the content that students are asked to learn tends to lead towards a pedagogy that embraces teacher-talk and deductive learning. Why would we spend time organising group work and activities that encourage interaction when doing so limits our capacity to constantly reinforce facts and figures that will be tested? So, a change in pedagogy to create more engaged students who will interact with knowledge and with their peers does not always align with how students will be tested. What is needed is for assessment to be refocused so that students are tested on their manipulation of information and synthesis of knowledge. This would lead to a greater emphasis in assessment (and in pedagogy) on developing students' capacity to answer the question, 'So what?'

There is also a need for a greater focus on understanding. Many experienced teachers will be in a position to modify their assignments in line with this thinking. However, many colleagues new to higher education will not yet be in a position to do this. So, how can we achieve the best for our students within the current system? By concentrating our teaching on helping students to develop the skills of critique, interrogation and comprehension. By improving our students' academic skills, they will be able to work out the answers for themselves, and in so doing they will start to enhance their wider understanding. We can cultivate these skills using both deductive and inductive approaches, and we can also reinforce the acquisition of academic skills by using the last phase of class as a time for reviewing what the students have learned, how they learned this and how the learning might be useful in future.

THE DIRECTION OF ASSESSMENT

Assessment doesn't only happen in one direction – students also ask 'What?' and 'So what?' of our teaching practice. The former is often easy to spot when we overhear students leaving the room saying things like, 'I didn't understand a word of that,' 'Wow, that was really interesting' or 'I finally understand what a genetic marker is.' It is harder to get a sense of the impact of our teaching – that is, how they will apply the concepts learned. This is why we need to consider the direction of assessment.

Most assessment involves the teacher giving feedback on students' work, but nowadays students provide feedback too. They are no longer passive recipients of knowledge; they are co-creators of their own learning experience. As educators, we want to develop student autonomy and for them to be engaged with their own learning. Students may have much to say but their voice is not always heard. Or, rather, their voice is heard but not always listened to. One of the ways we can attend to the student voice is through feedback. This can be done formally and informally through staff–student consultative committees, student evaluation questionnaires, the National Student Survey, consultations with academic advisers, discussion forums on VLEs, emails, ad-hoc chats in the corridor or coffee shop and so on. In this way, we can gain process *and* product reactions to our teaching practice.

Feedback from students is not an exact science because it is drawn from the specific experiences of individuals. Such data can be messy to gather and tricky to interpret, but that does not mean it should not be valued. The easy response to student feedback is to find errors in it. The difficult response is to recognise that what they are giving voice to is of genuine concern to them, and that it matters.

One of the problems with student feedback is that it is inclined to be qualitative rather than quantitative in nature. Quantitative feedback has the appearance of objectivity and seems generalisable, while qualitative data appears to be more subjective and contextually specific. This is a false dualism and has led to the reification of objectivity over experience. However, from the moment we start teaching in higher education, we realise the power of human engagement and the impact of interaction. For this reason, the assessment of the learning experience via student feedback is an important indicator of process learning.

As teachers, we will often offer qualitative feedback to our students, both written and verbal. If we want them to take such comments seriously, then we should learn to value qualitative feedback from them. Often teachers focus on one or two pieces of feedback – usually the super-positive or super-negative. Overly complimentary or overly critical appraisals are likely to be atypical, so we should aim to put them to one side and look for more general trends in the data and then act on commonly held perspectives.

EMBRACING SUBJECTIVITY

As we have seen, objectivity tends to have a higher status than subjectivity in academia, but this isn't universally true and it need not be true of student feedback. John Locke proposed that objects have primary and secondary qualities.[1] The primary qualities of an object are the properties that can be measured objectively: size, shape, number and so on. Secondary qualities relate to the way that we experience the world and involve our subjective interpretation of an object: colour, taste, sound and so on. This dichotomy represents the separation of objectivity and experience. We can see this in the art world where a painting is not assessed by its size but by something much less tangible.

---

1   J. Locke, *An Essay Concerning Human Understanding* (London: Penguin, 1997 [1689]).

Visitors to the Louvre typically spend three hours in the museum and follow a well-worn path, taking in the *Venus de Milo*, the *Mona Lisa* and *The Wounded Cuirassier*.[2] As they huddle together at the *Mona Lisa*, with its estimated value of over £1 billion, visitors are often struck by how small it is (77cm x 53cm). If the *Mona Lisa* were valued only for its primary qualities then we could easily cost the price of some oil paints, a wooden panel and a nice oak frame. We could even factor in the hourly rate of the artist, trans-portation costs, marketing expenses and any mark-up added by intermediaries. You don't need a calculator to see that it is unlikely to add up to £1 billion; therefore, we must assume that the value of the *Mona Lisa* is based on its secondary qualities. There is an argument that the worth of any object is simply what someone is willing to pay for it, but this too is driven by subjective factors.

Higher education has primary qualities. Degrees are divided into years; years are made up of various units; lectures last for a certain amount of time, as do tutorials, seminars and classes; exams are timed; essays have word counts; and the final output is a degree classification. But students are not automatons who move through the system like robots. Students do not just *attend* a lecture, they experience it. Students do not just *sit* an exam, they experience it. Students do not just *go* to university, they experience it. In fact, the secondary qualities of higher education are the central facets, so when students feed back their subjective insights we should listen to them.

The value of feedback from students lies in the centrality of their experience. Being a student is a primary experi-ence infused with secondary qualities. Autonomous

---

2   Y. Yoshimura, S. Sobolevsky, C. Ratti, F. Girardin, J. P. Carrascal, J. Blat and R. Sinatra, An Analysis of Visitors' Behavior in the Louvre Museum: A Study Using Bluetooth Data. *Environment and Planning B: Planning and Design*, 41(6) (2014): 1113-1131.

students must be supported in developing and embracing their own experiences in the teaching and learning environment, and one of the ways of doing this is by valuing the student voice, which we can begin to do by engaging with them. Student feedback can be a rather blunt tool, but it is made blunter still if we simply reduce it to data sets for institutional reports. Taking feedback seriously can help us to generate a virtuous cycle which recognises the subjectivity of experience while simultaneously understanding that experience is central to the human condition. Quantifying the higher education experience lessens its worth, but listening to the student voice enables us to appreciate its qualitative value.

THREE CHALLENGES

1 **Try to see feedback as a learning tool.** Feedback has become a rather generic term – it covers specific actions such as praise, grade, feedforward, comment, critique and challenge. Instead of thinking about feedback as a form of communication between you and your students, aim to think about it as a learning tool – concentrate on the impact of your feedback and how it will improve students' future learning. Take a moment to reflect on whether you are happy with your feedback balance – whether it is too positive, too negative or too vague. When people say they are giving 'constructive feedback' they sometimes err on the negative and actually give destructive feedback. Likewise, offering cursory statements such as 'Well done' is not really giving feedback at all as there is no utility in this type of statement. It is important to say things like 'Well done', 'Great' or 'Terrific', of course, but these statements are not feedback – they are praise.

Feedback needs to be focused and useful. It needs to be based on facts, positive expectations and realistic strategies for success. When giving face-to-face feedback try to make sure that the student says more than you do. Use evidence-based statements to question, probe and prompt. And don't be afraid of a few awkward silences. The best way to give written feedback is to imagine you are saying it directly to the student. It needs to be honest, fair, developmental and human. Remember that feedback isn't just an account of what has happened; feedback is a facilitator of learning. If our feedback doesn't offer students explicit steps towards future success, then they will simply hear implicit negative messages.

2 **Try to ask questions that focus on critical thinking rather than on knowledge retention.** Let's aspire to limit the number of questions that ask students to regurgitate information and to start asking more probing questions – for example, 'Why?' is better than 'What?' When asking questions, try to start with 'How' (How does ...?, How would ...?, How might ...?). These question strings support critical thinking because they suggest that there are many possible answers and the students have to work out what they think will work best. Questioning can be a great tool for demonstrating to students that you expect them to work in a critical manner, but you need to be careful in how you use questions. Starting the class with a few simple closed questions may seem like a good idea but it can actually set the wrong tone – the students may think that in today's class you are looking for 'right' answers. Starting with more abstract questions suggests that 'Today we will be thinking!'

When students respond to your questions, try to offer follow-up questions such as, 'Tell me why you think ...'

and 'What are the strengths and weaknesses of your answer?' This will help them to see that you are not just interested in their answer but in how they formulate their answer. This can be further developed if you challenge students to respond to your questions with a question of their own. Student-generated questions are one of the indicators of a safe learning environment: if they feel comfortable enough to ask you questions, then you have established a good learning space. Some people think that when students ask questions it means they want answers, but that is only half right. It also means they trust you enough to question you. Don't answer student questions until at least one student has volunteered their answer. When students stay behind after class to ask you questions, it tells you two things: (1) there is a gap in their understanding and (2) you have created a positive environment in which it's OK to ask questions and students are aware of their own learning journey.

Finally, it is important that you don't answer your own questions. If there is no answer from the students, then rephrase the question, wait, rephrase again and then move on. This might feel slightly uncomfortable for some students who might feel a lack of closure if they haven't been given an answer – but if they want closure then they will need to ask for it! Remember that it is not the teacher's job to give answers; it is the teacher's job to help their students develop the skills so that they are able to find answers for themselves.

3 **Try to encourage metacognition.** Learning is clearly important, but metacognition involves reflecting on how we learn – our learning strategies and processes. Many students will have developed their own implicit techniques, but if you can help them to examine their metacognitive processes, then you can encourage

them to make more active use of them later on. Your task here is to help the students to see how they have come to learn something, so they can use similar methods in future learning – otherwise, learning can be rather haphazard. You can support metacognition in two ways. Firstly, by sharing your own strategies and encouraging students to examine how they have learned something. This has nothing to do with learning styles (there is no research evidence to support the notion of visual, auditory or kinaesthetic learning styles); rather, it is a chance to sit back and examine the methodology behind their answers. A phrase that I hear myself use is, 'The way I remember this is ...' Feel free to share your strategies in this way too. However, the second option – student-generated strategies – is probably more effective. After introducing a tricky new concept, ask the students to work in pairs (four minutes) to review how they are going to remember the concept they have learned. Then ask them to share their strategies with each other. Do this regularly so the students build up a range of learning strategies and see learning as an active process.

LITTLE NUGGETS OF WISDOM

INTERACTION

- Successful interactive learning involves student-to-student, student-to-teacher and student-to-activity engagement.

- When a student makes a great point in class say something like, 'That's a brilliant point! Now I want everyone to pair up and work out three reasons why I like that point so much.'

- After class, reflect on who did all the talking and who didn't contribute to the whole-class discussion. If it is always the same students, then you might need to try a few new teaching strategies.

- Take a step back and look around the room when a student answers your question. This will help the rest of the group to feel involved.

- A question-and-answer session is not the best way to generate discussion because the students might feel you are testing them or looking for specific answers; it is better to present hypotheses, offer two counterpoints or play devil's advocate.

TASKS

- Don't expect the students to be able to answer your questions instantly. A good response needs some thinking time. For knowledge-based questions this could just be five seconds, but for conceptual and analytical questions they may need 30–60 seconds.

- Giving students more time to complete a task doesn't necessarily mean that the results will be better. Clear direction and shared success criteria are more likely to help achieve the desired outcome.

- Halfway through a long activity, ask the students to pause and review the task guidelines. This is an especially useful intervention during group work, during which early discussions can often lead students off task.

- When students are doing short tasks (less than seven minutes), stay back and let them get on with it themselves.

- When students are giving feedback after a task, don't feel the need to unpack all their comments. If you think they would benefit from a point being elaborated on, then simply say, 'That's really interesting, tell me more.'

ASSESSMENT

- Assessment is an educational tool that seeks to support a student's future learning rather than simply judge their current status.

- A good assessment task doesn't just test for what is known; it should also test for what is unknown.

- Assessment shouldn't be the end of learning. Try to see assessment as something that is beneficial to students' future learning.

- Grades are not the best measure of learning. True learning is about increased understanding, personal empowerment and an enhanced sense of humanity.

- Encourage students to assess the impact of the activities you ask them to complete and report back on what worked for them, and why.

CHAPTER 4

OBSERVATION AS A LEARNING PROCESS

The observation of teaching is a structured and effective pedagogical tool that can help to improve the quality of teaching in higher education institutions.[1] By being observed and, in turn, observing others, implicit aspects of teaching practice can be examined and made explicit and areas in need of refinement can be identified. Most of my development as a teacher in higher education has come from observing others and reflecting. Therefore, rather than seeing observation as a form of scrutiny or assessment to which we are subjected, it is better to think of it as a shared learning tool.

Often, when we think of observation, we think of being observed, but it is just as important to consider the importance of observing others. Observation in this regard becomes a learning process, conducted by peers with the intention of supporting each other to develop. So, whether you are being observed or whether you are observing a colleague, try to see observation as a development tool.

Peer observation is underpinned by a number of key principles:

● Everyone involved is an equal partner.

---

1   G. D. Henry and G. R. Oliver, Seeing is Believing: The Benefits of Peer Observation. *Journal of University Teaching and Learning Practice*, 9(1) (2012), article 7.

- The process is transparent.

- The focus is on development.

- Dialogue is integral to the process.

- The process should be mutually beneficial.

- The focus of the observation should be agreed beforehand.

- The significance of the learning context is key.

- There should be shared ownership of the process.

- Peers should not position themselves as expert educators.

- Student learning must not be negatively affected by the observation process.

- Pre- and post-observation meetings are just as important as the actual observation.

It is also beneficial to consider which perspective you will be observing from and how you see your role as an observer. Some people like to sit 'outside' the activity and observe from a neutral perspective, but you can also learn a lot from joining in and doing the tasks the students are asked to carry out. In order to find the right balance, it is a good idea to have a pre-observation chat with your colleague over a cup of tea and work out how best to proceed. You could also discuss key areas that you should focus on or any new activities that are being tried out for the first time on which they would like particular feedback.

Consider observing from the student perspective. In this example, teacher A observes teacher B by being part of the class, not by sitting outside the activity as an 'objective' observer.

USING OBSERVATION TO FIND THE UNDERPINNINGS OF TEACHING

Clearly, everyone who teaches in higher education has their own approach to teaching. They may have learned the ways of their subject through their own studies, practical experience or reflective practice. For some, their pedagogical approach has been carefully constructed through the scrutiny of education theory and the critical reading of educational literature. Many develop their practice by studying towards formal qualifications. But there are also a great many individuals who have developed their skills tacitly and built their understanding of teaching through direct on-the-job experience.

Observing and being observed also provides objective input that can improve your practice. Cultivating the ability to sit outside your own pedagogical practice is a powerful tool, but it is not always easy in a busy environment and some factors might get overlooked. Being observed helps you to refine your practice through constructive and purposeful reflection and feedback. Feedback from a colleague's observations will help you to check your assumptions and give you a new 'teacher' perspective on how your students engage with the learning experience. Likewise, when you are observing a colleague, you will have the capacity to shine a light on the things they implicitly do and, in doing so, help your peer to examine what they do and why they do it. Peer observation is about uncovering the processes and underpinning structures of your teaching.

The beauty of peer observation is that it provides you with an opportunity to consider the teaching event from two perspectives. First, you can explore the students' learning experience by focusing on the clarity of the teaching, the core messages and the methods used to engage the students in their learning. However, as a peer, you are also able to place yourself in your colleague's shoes and try to work out why they have taken one approach over another. Subsequent post-observation chats can then be used to confirm whether you got a good handle on this or whether there were other factors behind their pedagogical choices. This discussion will also help you to make explicit to your colleague some of those 'automatic pilot' moments that we all slip into when we are unaware of our actions. This dual viewpoint enables you to experience both the surface teaching/learning event and also gain some insight into the underpinning rationale and justification.

Consider putting yourself in the shoes of the colleague you are observing. This will help you to move from a mindset of judgement to one where you see your role as developmental – for both of you. Here, teacher A observes teacher B from the student's perspective as well as from teacher B's perspective.

THE UNDERPINNING PRINCIPLES OF PEER OBSERVATION

Quinlan and Åkerlind suggest that the peer observation process relies on 'collegial conversations and collaborations about teaching, rather than merely ... peer judgments about teaching'.[2] Peers should aim to have discussions

---

2   K. Quinlan and G. Åkerlind, Factors Affecting Departmental Peer Collaboration for Faculty Development: Two Cases in Context. *Higher Education*, 40(1) (2000): 23-52 at 27.

before and after the observation, and both partners should seek to find specific areas for development. During initial discussions or in setting subsequent action plans, there is no point in dwelling on details that cannot be modified (curriculum, environment, student body, etc.). Instead, the focus should be on identifying elements that can be realistically changed in the short, medium and long term. This may include (but is not limited to):

● Clarity of explanation.

● Use of questions.

● Suitability of anecdotes.

● Organisation of student activity.

● Interaction with students.

Peer observation is a dialogic partnership – both before and after the observation. The observation process may also support collegial discussion in the longer term.

THE RULES OF ENGAGEMENT

Sometimes observers become so intrigued by the topic the observee is teaching that they start to focus on the content rather than the pedagogy. This is especially true when the observer and the observee are both based in the same discipline. In this instance, the observer can easily become caught up in the subject matter as they will have the disciplinary knowledge to examine it in a detailed and thoughtful way. One way to overcome this – and a great way to expand beyond your own signature pedagogy – is to observe colleagues from many different fields and subject areas. In this way, the examination of content is reduced through your own legitimate ignorance and there can be a greater focus on the act of teaching itself.

The role of the observer is to be a critical friend who identifies areas of strength and areas for further development. The feedback they offer should always be a conduit for academic development. Both the observer and the observee should benefit: the observer becomes more skilled at examining the factors that make up successful teaching and learning experiences, and the observee is given specific feedback on how to develop their practice.

ACTION PLANS

Peer observation aims to develop the teaching practice of both the observer and the observee through a supportive and formative review of current pedagogy.

Peer observation is a two-way process.

At its most basic, peer observation involves one colleague observing another and offering constructive feedback; however, the emphasis should fall not on the observation phase of this process but on the discussion that follows. The collegial approach means that insights and ideas for improvement can be shared, enabling both participants to enhance the quality of their teaching.[3] The purpose of this dialogue is to develop a realistic and achievable action plan that the observee can act on to improve their practice. The best action plans are usually short, direct and feature two or three areas for development – for example:

● Try to record key terms that you use by writing a list on the board and encouraging students to copy these down with their own definitions.

● If you decide to join a group of students, sit down with them rather than tower over them.

3   M. Bell, Supported Reflective Practice: A Programme of Peer Observation and Feedback for Academic Teaching Development. *International Journal for Academic Development*, 6(1) (2001): 26–39.

- Avoid repeating too much information for students who arrive late.

- One group finished five minutes before the other groups; try to consider extension tasks for groups who finish early.

SEARCHLIGHT AND SPOTLIGHT OBSERVATIONS

Teaching in the spotlight

Some observations deliberately place the spotlight on particular aspects of teaching practice. The observee asks the observer to concentrate on these parts of their teaching.

A searchlight on teaching

Some observations take a more searching approach and shine a broad light on the observee's teaching practice to help home in on specific areas that need further attention.

Shining a *spotlight* on specific features of teaching practice often means that the resulting action plan is easier to develop, more focused and more detailed. However, sometimes the observee does not find it easy to identify particular aspects of their teaching that they wish to be observed, so they might ask the observer to take a broader look at their practice. The *searchlight* approach to observation involves an evaluation of the entirety of the teaching session with the aim of finding two or three broad areas for further development. The feedback and action plan are likely to be less detailed than one produced for a spotlight observation, and might even result in a follow-up observation that concentrates only on the highlighted areas. Both types of observation have their merits, and the peers involved might even decide to adopt a mixed model. However, the observee should always take the lead when deciding on the focus for the observation and the target should always be to work towards an achievable action plan.

Here is peer observation in a nutshell:

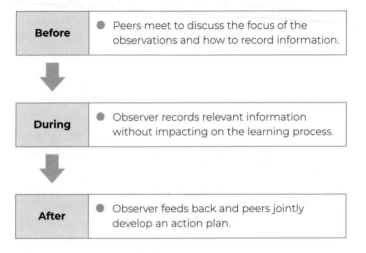

Before	● Peers meet to discuss the focus of the observations and how to record information.
During	● Observer records relevant information without impacting on the learning process.
After	● Observer feeds back and peers jointly develop an action plan.

THREE MODELS OF PEER OBSERVATION

The main ways to organise peer observation are as a pair or small group or at a departmental level. Two colleagues could simply get together to work as a pair: they could agree on the process between themselves and keep their feedback and actions contained within their pair. The peers might come from the same department but they could just as easily come from different departments. Working with peers from the same department means there is a level of shared understanding from the start and colleagues will have relatively easy access to one another;

however, the process might become rather insular, with certain areas over-examined and other areas under-examined. If peers are from different departments they are more likely to focus on the process of teaching rather than the content. The same is true if peers work as a small group: colleagues can come from one department or from a number of departments (although it might be a bit awkward if only one individual is from a different department).

Peer observation can also be done at a whole-department level, in which case a carousel approach is used, with each person observing and feeding back to the next person in the chain. This method is usually more structured because, in general, the more people involved, the more organised the system needs to be, and the less personal it becomes. The real benefit of working as a collective is that it gives status and kudos to the activity, and this often means that resources are more likely to be obtained for development.

There is no 'right' way to organise a peer observation pro-cess. Colleagues should consider the make-up of the group and whether the focus will be on teaching within their own field or developing generic teaching skills. Over the following two pages I highlight some of the strengths and weaknesses of three models of peer observation.

PAIRED OBSERVATION

Pros	Cons
Easy to organise and timetable.	Hard to find the 'right' partner.
Helps to build collegial bonds.	Doesn't carry much institutional weight.
Easy to maintain a low-key approach.	Limited to the professional insight of the two individuals.

SMALL GROUP OBSERVATION

Pros	Cons
Widens the scope of input.	Might be tempted to value one individual's input over the others'.
Helps to develop a supportive network.	Having more people doesn't necessarily mean there is an increased benefit; it could just be more of the same.
Different individuals will be able to identify different aspects of teaching practice.	

DEPARTMENTAL/COLLECTIVE OBSERVATION

Pros	Cons
A range of expertise and input.	Not everyone will be equally committed.
Can lead to departmental/institutional change through the weight of evidence.	Can become institutionalised.
Each individual might get the chance to learn from many colleagues.	Large groups can be difficult to manage and maintain.
	The individual might be overlooked.

LEARNING THROUGH FEEDBACK

There is so much to be learned from peer observations – from the process itself, from the subsequent debriefing and from any written feedback. If you have decided to give written feedback, it is important that you engage with this in a positive way. As we have seen, both the observer and the observee need to focus on this being a meeting of two colleagues who are seeking to develop rather than judge.

What follows are three examples of feedback, which are written from the perspective of the observer and are intended to be read by the observee (rather than institutional documents intended to be part of a quality enhancement process). I am not claiming that these are exemplars or that they represent a gold standard; instead, I am presenting them as positive, formative and observational illustrations. Observational feedback is often given using a pro forma or in reference to pre-established criteria, but these examples are written in open prose. However, although there is no set structure, similar themes are evident – such as the structure, of teaching, levels of student-interaction and the generally upbeat tone. Have a read through and see if you can find any pointers (or nuggets) that could help with the development of your own practice.

OBSERVATION EXAMPLE 1

SUMMARY

You started the session with a quick review of what was learned previously and what was to be examined in this session. Your general manner and approach were such that you came across as being relaxed, informed and in control. Your body language was open and you used the pitch and cadence of your voice to emphasise key points. You scanned the classroom throughout and made an effort to share eye contact with the students. You asked good questions and you offered clear and thoughtful explanations. When asking a higher-level question there was no initial answer, so you toned down the question and asked the students first of all to offer a definition. This worked well and was a good idea – by starting with a question that involved justification and analysis, you allowed yourself room to adapt the question to one that involved definition. Your initial question was suitable for students at this level, but by toning it down you made it clear that you were looking for an answer before you moved on. You seemed in control and your use of praise and feedback reinforced your role as the supportive expert in the room.

STRUCTURE OF SESSION

The session had four main phases: introduction, background to literary theory, key theoretical figures, and core issues with literary theory. All of these phases used the same teaching model. Of 25 students, all seemed busy taking notes throughout the session but only five were actively involved in questioning/discussion. You may wish to consider using a few different teaching approaches (group work, debate, student presentation, etc.) to offer a variety of ways for students to engage with the material. Students find it difficult to concentrate at a sustained level for two hours, and changing your approach can help to increase the levels of engagement and focus.

The first phase looked at literary theory. This was done through a step-by-step explanation which was supported by a clear and purposeful PowerPoint. After this initial overview you asked questions to try to encourage deeper learning. The students were rather reticent and preferred to take notes, but two students engaged with you (their responses showed a good understanding and you clarified any points that needed it). You may wish to think about seeking questions during teacher-led explanations – your default position was to cover an entire topic then ask some questions or seek questions from the group. It was evident that you are quite skilful in your questioning and you tended to use higher-order questions that pushed students to give justifications rather than just offer simple answers. You could use these skills by breaking up explanations and interspersing them with questions that ask students why X was done or not done.

For the most part the students were focused on taking notes (mainly using laptops). This meant that their heads were down, which limited the level of eye contact you could share with them. The result of this was that, when you asked a question, only some students looked up to catch your eye and only a small percentage of them felt able to offer an answer. This shouldn't be seen as being a result of your practice – in fact, you asked really good questions and offered students praise for their responses. The problem here is a mismatch between teaching approaches and learning approaches, and in order for this to change you may wish to alter the format of the learning by introducing activities that will encourage students to work away from their screens. Since the four phases of the session followed a similar format, the students' ways of responding will also stick to this structure and it will be hard for you to get the level of verbal engagement you desire if they are working in this way. Overall, the students were taking lots of notes and were focused, but they were not very interactive.

PowerPoint was your main visual tool and this was clear and easy to follow. The font was the right size and could be read from the back of the room. However, it was hard to see the bottom half of the screen from the back (because the seats are not ramped); therefore you may wish to look at how you could move the writing on your PowerPoints so the key points are in the top half of the screen. This point was not so important for the students with laptops as they all had copies of the PowerPoint, but those working with notepads may have missed some points. Overall, the layout and content of the PowerPoint was spot on but you may wish to consider sight lines (the ability to see the screen).

MOVING FORWARD

Overall, your teaching showed ability and structure. You worked in an open and friendly manner and your delivery had a nice balance of explanation, example, links to specific aspects of theory and links to specific texts. I would suggest that you focus your reflections on supporting more students to interact with the material and with your questions. The ability to critique, examine and justify are core skills, so developing a teaching model that nourishes such skills may be a good idea. You clearly have ability and with some reflection and appropriate action planning you will develop your pedagogy yet further.

OBSERVATION EXAMPLE 2

SUMMARY

The session started with you offering a brief, shared overview covering the key aspects of the session. There was then a quick whole-class recap on previous activities – 'What happened?' and 'How did you feel?' Then the students were divided into groups and each group examined a specific resource. There was a technical problem with a video clip, so you decided to continue with three sources rather than four. This was a good idea. You tried to fix the sound problem but, rightly, decided to give up rather than spend time on this. The groups then worked on the resources – following three set questions. There was a high level of student engagement in the group work, but perhaps you could consider giving the tasks timeframes so there is a greater sense of focus and ask the students to feed back in relation to specific questions rather than just asking them for general feedback. That said, the feedback and discussion was quite rich and a number of voices were heard.

STRUCTURE OF THE SESSION

During the initial group work you moved around the room and offered support as required – in doing so, you offered a good balance of support so as not to leave groups reliant on your input. Your manner during the feedback was open and you were keen to allow students to offer their perspectives. You offered broad praise for their input, and when the students were not forthcoming you asked supplemental questions. This was well done and it kept the emphasis on them being active rather than you giving them the answers. While the questioning worked well, you might want to reflect on how you could ask more probing questions: 'Can you tell me more about X?', 'Why do you think that?', 'How does that relate to Y?'

The next phase of the session involved a free writing task that mirrored a task the students had done at the start of the course. This was a great idea and was well received by the students. Once again, you gave them space to complete the task and you made it clear that this was a safe space for them to write honestly. You could have given them a little longer to complete this task (it might be helpful here for you to reflect on giving tasks appropriate timeframes and sharing these with the students). Once again, there was some whole-class feedback and discussion and once again this was rich and purposeful. You were good at pulling together key points and you offered further clarification when needed. You are good at drawing out points from those students who are most comfortable speaking in whole-class situations, but you may want to think about ways of getting perspectives from students who do not feel so confident. Perhaps you could make use of written feedback on whiteboards or sticky notes? In the closing stage of the session you showed a short video and asked some questions about it in relation to key themes. This was helpful in pulling together key aspects of the session.

There was whole-class discussion at various points in the session and there was also group work. Both of these allowed the students to work in a supported environment and there was a good level of participation overall. The instructions to the students in the first task were a little vague and could have been more clearly stated, but they enjoyed the tasks and worked in a purposeful manner. Students from each group fed back and you asked supplemental and prompting questions. During the whole-class discussion some students gave more input than others (which is to be expected). The level of discussion was high and it was obvious that the students had engaged with the key concepts. Perhaps during these discussion phases you could try to encourage more cross-class analysis – for example, after hearing one student's feedback you might praise them and then ask another student to offer a counter-position. Alternatively, you could ask another student to 'piggyback' on a good piece of feedback – for example: 'That's a good point – can anyone think of a reason why some people might reject this?' or 'That's a great point – can anyone tell me why that is such a good idea?'

All the students were involved at some stage of the session and they were focused throughout. You managed the tasks well and you facilitated discussions. With a few small tweaks you could start to push the students to be more analytical about their own and their peers' comments. Your manner was clearly aligned to the course content and the field in general. You showed that you valued the students' perspectives and you allowed them to feel safe in the learning environment. You rightly avoided giving them mini-lectures and instead allowed them to work through things for themselves.

MOVING FORWARD

Perhaps you could reflect on your use of your voice – you have a tendency to fade out at the end of questions and you also ask multi-string questions. You may wish to consider asking one clear question and using your voice to punctuate/add emphasis at the end of the question. You may also wish to consider where you stand/sit in the classroom. You do seem relaxed and this relaxes the students and allows them to feel confident to talk, but sitting on a table can restrict your voice projection, so it is worth thinking about when you stand, when you sit and how you hold yourself. Overall, you seemed in control and you have a subdued confidence that was suitable for this group, but there are a few things you could do that might help you to project your voice to the furthest student and ask questions that are more direct.

On the whole, this was a successful session and it was evident that learning happened. Your students clearly appreciate you – probably because you give them time/space to offer their perspectives. The resources and tasks were well thought out and the balance between group work and whole-class work allowed all the students to be involved at some stage. With reflection on using timeframes, asking single-string questions, asking more probing questions and projecting your voice you will enhance your current good practice. It is clear that you have a talent for teaching in this environment – try to reflect on what you think is best about your teaching (I found many areas that I liked) and try to reflect on two or three small changes that you could introduce to enhance things further.

OBSERVATION EXAMPLE 3

SUMMARY

The class started with a brief introduction but there was no clear sharing of learning expectations. It is true that not all groups need to be given intended learning outcomes at the start of a session but these can offer a useful framework for learning – and it later became clear that this group might benefit from such explicit frameworks. There was then a student presentation that lasted almost 30 minutes, which seems rather too long and meant that other students were somewhat passive for the first third of the class. There was then 30 minutes of whole-class discussion. This allowed some members of the class to contribute but others remained silent. The most vibrant part of the session was the group activity which followed, where two groups were asked to examine a scenario from different perspectives. This task worked well – everyone seemed engaged and there was some good critical debate within the groups. After some feedback, the class was drawn to a close and the students left.

STRUCTURE OF SESSION

This was a 90-minute class, so there was space for the group to reflect on what they had learned at the end – a student-led plenary would have offered a good closure technique. Overall, the presentation and the discussion were rather lengthy and excluded certain students, whereas the group work was more structured and allowed everyone to contribute. It might be worthwhile reflecting on making some activities shorter, offering more opportunities for group work, and giving tasks more explicit frameworks within which students can debate/discuss and relate to one another.

During the lengthy presentation there was no interaction and as it closed you asked if there were any questions. There were none. I think this was a function of the presentation itself. Perhaps you could ask students to write down questions during the presentation, then you could pick a few at random at the end. Perhaps presenters could also be given clearer guidance on what they should cover and how long they should take. The whole-class discussion mainly involved three students with small contributions from four others. But six students did not contribute. You asked good critical questions but the students mainly gave their responses to you and rarely debated as a group. Again, a more structured approach might help with class discussion. Perhaps you could ask the group to discuss three core concepts (written on the board or a handout) which you could refer back to during the discussion and keep a check on whether they have all been covered in enough detail. You could also pause the debate at times and ask all the students to write down one key point and one question on a sticky note and stick these on the wall. At the end of the debate you could select some at random and ask for further clarification from its author; in this way you can also keep an eye on who writes the questions and be selective in your choices.

The most successful phase of the session was the group work where they worked in two groups to examine a scenario from two perspectives. This worked well and everyone seemed involved. This activity also encouraged them to debate their group responses and offer differing opinions in a relatively safe space. At the end of the group work one of the students who had not contributed during the whole-class discussion was the first to speak and offered some insightful comments. This suggests that group work can be a good place to generate ideas and that it might have been better if the group work had followed the presentation (i.e. before the whole-class discussion). There was clear evidence that the students were familiar with the literature and they offered some good opinions. However, they could have been pushed a little more to be critical with this knowledge. Perhaps you could have given them approaches/tools for examining this content knowledge. For example, in the group work they could have been asked to examine the topics through specific lenses (power, poverty, ethics, ethnicity, etc.). There could then have been some discussion on the benefits of examining content through a certain lens.

The whiteboard was used in two ways: to present a model and to record student feedback from the group task. There was also a PowerPoint slideshow to generate the group work. This usage was clear and purposeful. Your handwriting was a little messy and you might consider two techniques: (1) try to write from your shoulder (not your wrist), aiming to write quite large, flowing letters, and (2) when collating student feedback you could ask a member of another group to write it on the board. This second option will help the students to synthesise answers into succinct bullet points, and if everyone is given a chance to do this over the term they will all benefit from learning the skill of synthesising knowledge.

MOVING FORWARD

The class ended rather suddenly without a plenary. It is hard to have a plenary when there are no clear learning outcomes or class aims, but they can offer an opportunity for students to review what they have learned from the session. Perhaps you could simply ask them to turn to their neighbour and discuss two things they have learned and one thing they need to investigate further. This could then be shared with the class and might help you to focus on what you need to teach less/more of in future. You may also wish to reflect on the skills the students may/may not develop as a result of attending the class – do they simply get the opportunity to show what they already know, or do you get the chance to offer them new tools/ approaches that they can use to critically analyse content?

Overall, it is clear that you have many natural talents that will benefit you and your class. You show a student-centred perspective, you ask good questions and you come across as someone who is in control but approachable. I think that taking your current abilities and framing them within a more purposeful teaching/learning structure will enable you to make the most of your natural ability.

The feedback that is developed from observations is a rich source of pedagogical development. It can sometimes be hard to hear what others have to say about our teaching because it is quite a personal activity, but it is also important to remember that it is not the way that we present our teaching that is important, but the way that it is received. Teaching happens for the benefit of learning, so while we might feel that we have done a great job in structuring our session, ultimately its success will be judged by others.

THREE CHALLENGES

1   **Try to see teaching as a constant cycle of improvement.** As higher education changes, some people complain that those who teach in it are now expected to be all-singing, all-dancing practitioners. I think that is wrong: I expect students to be all-singing, all-dancing learners! Our job is to keep our practice under review, so we can ensure that our students are truly learning. People talk about learning to teach as if it were a finite process. Don't try to be the best teacher, just try to be better every time you teach. We call it *teaching practice*, not *teaching perfect*, so keep your focus on development and improvement.

Good teaching is an active commitment to enhancing your students' learning experience. Observation and feedback give you the opportunity to stop and question your practice with the hope of improving it. As well as getting good observational data from peers, you could also consider getting feedback on your teaching from the students themselves. If you are trying out a new teaching/learning activity and it goes wrong, don't be afraid to share this with the class. Tell them what you hoped for and ask them to explain why it didn't work and how they think the task could be improved next time.

2   **Try to consider how you use visual aids.** The two main types of visual aid used in whole-class teaching are whiteboards (for writing on) and PowerPoints (for presenting information). The former is a more interactive tool and is great 'in the moment'. The latter is useful as it allows you to plan how you will present information beforehand. When writing on the board, try to write from your shoulder and keep your writing sufficiently big and legible so that students in the back row can read what you have written. It is a waste of time writing something that no one can read, so keep your eye on how you communicate information to the students.

A good rule of thumb with PowerPoint is to assume that your presentation is too long and your slides too wordy. Before the lesson, try sitting at the back of the classroom and run through your slides. Are the slides mainly text? Is the text too small? Do the colours clash? Are your slides just dull? If the answer to any of these questions is yes, then you need to revise your slides. Also, if time is running out, it is better to skip to the last of your slides – rushing to get through everything helps no one. If your PowerPoint presentation is really your teaching notes, then something has gone wrong! Cut the visual aids and only use slides to add emphasis to specific points. Remember that visual aids are merely conduits and are additional to learning – the real learning takes place between you and the students and between the students and their peers.

3 **Try to be open to the perspectives of others.** Peer observation is not a 'natural' aspect of teaching in higher education. For the most part, we engage with our students by ourselves, without other colleagues around. But inviting a colleague to observe you, or being invited to observe a colleague, can be a fantastic pedagogical development process. The secret is to be open to feedback and to offer your own feedback as points for consideration. Feedback needs to be focused on possible utility – there is no point in discussing factors that cannot be changed. Utility can come from positive and negative feedback. It is great to hear good things about your teaching, but try to examine what you can *do* with this positive information. It is harder to hear about areas of your practice that are not so strong, but this type of analysis is often easier to act on.

One element of feedback that is often overlooked (but is actually very important) is the 'neutral' stuff that we do – the things that are neither good nor bad. We tend to be preoccupied by the negative and flattered by the positive, but some aspects of practice are fundamental to the whole process, such as creating resources, organising groups, having the right artefacts and so on. Don't overlook the everyday aspects of practice!

Whatever type of feedback you receive, make sure you think about how to act on it. Don't be defensive. Instead of offering justification and rationale for what you have done, ask your observer what they think you can do next time to improve. Observation and feedback are part of an iterative cycle, but we need to be open to hearing critical comments before we can truly act on them.

LITTLE NUGGETS OF WISDOM

REFLECTION

- It is easier to change one teacher than it is to change 30 students. Developing your own practice makes quantitative and qualitative sense.

- Experiential learning involves reflecting on two questions: 'What have I been doing?' and 'What can I do better?' The students can do this about their learning and you can do this about your teaching.

- The best students are not necessarily the 'brightest' students; the best students are the ones who make you think and push you to improve.

- We need to learn to take a step back and examine teaching from another point of view.

- Try to reflect on different dimensions of your teaching practice and set specific targets against each individual aspect.

DEVELOPMENT

- Remember that learning is a choice. Consider how you can show evidence of good teaching practice so that students choose to engage with your teaching.

- Listening to our students and peers gives us a unique learning-centred perspective on how to develop our pedagogy.

- Try to see teaching as a learning activity that is always in need of improvement.

- Education has a kinetic quality: the more you actively engage, the more charged up you become, and the more you get out.

- When you get feedback on your teaching practice, try to divide your actions into short-, medium- and long-term activities.

ACTIONS

- When students are presenting to the class, sit in their vacant seat. Don't hover at their shoulder drawing the attention of the class.

- Try to limit teacher-talk when writing on the board. Students will either read the board or listen, but they won't do both.

- Use your 'teacher voice' to emphasise expected student activity – your tone can indicate focus, vibrancy, engagement, interaction and much more.

- Avoid starting questions with phrases such as, 'Who can tell me ...?' or 'Does anyone know ...?' These phrases turn answering a question into a competition.

- Try to talk a little less each time you teach.

CHAPTER 5

LOOKING BACK, GOING FORWARD

The trouble with doing stuff is twofold. First of all, whatever stuff you plan to do is much more achievable if you believe there is going to be a positive outcome. Secondly, it is much more likely that you will be successful if you choose to do easy stuff. This is not to say that you shouldn't attempt to do difficult and/or pointless stuff, it's just that doing hard stuff can be a real effort and sometimes we might want some easy wins. In this chapter, I will explore a straightforward way of enhancing teaching practice – reflective practice – and, in particular, everyday reflective practice.

The concept of reflective practice has been around for a long time and finds its roots in the work of Donald Schön. For Schön, reflection is an explicit and conscious analysis of practice in an attempt to understand what is currently happening and how it can be improved. Schön's *Educating the Reflective Practitioner* is the cornerstone of reflective practice,[1] but it isn't necessarily an easy read and he doesn't offer much guidance about how we might actually go about being reflective practitioners. For a more accessible introduction, I would recommend Jennifer Moon's *Reflection in Learning and Professional Development*.[2]

---

1   D. A. Schön, *Educating the Reflective Practitioner: Toward a New Design for Teaching and Learning in the Professions* (San Francisco, CA: Jossey-Bass, 1987).

2   J. A. Moon, *Reflection in Learning and Professional Development: Theory and Practice* (Abingdon and New York: Routledge, 2013).

There have been many proposals about how to enact reflective practice in higher education in order to enhance teaching practice: Boud suggests using journal writing,[3] Williams and Jacobs suggest reflection through blogs[4] and Ryan recommends adopting systematic reflective writing practices.[5] The trouble with all these approaches is that they involve doing stuff that is not central to everyday higher education teaching practice. A model of everyday reflective practice is more likely to be successful if it has a close and clear connection with what happens in the classroom and seems to be doable within the confines of the teaching and learning environment.

A FRAMEWORK FOR REFLECTIVE PRACTICE

In teaching (and in research) I tend to ask two questions: 'What?' and 'So what?' (as we saw in Chapter 3). The first of these seeks to discover what is happening, while the second looks for possible impact. The beauty of these questions is their simplicity and portability. After a heated meeting I can walk away asking myself, 'What happened there?' and 'What am I going to do about it?' After reading a journal article I can think to myself, 'What are the key messages?' and 'How do these translate to my world?' After a successful class, I can reflect on what made it successful and how I can maximise this in the future (likewise,

---

3   D. Boud, Using Journal Writing to Enhance Reflective Practice. *New Directions for Adult and Continuing Education*, 90 (2001): 9-18.

4   J. B. Williams and J. S. Jacobs, Exploring the Use of Blogs As Learning Spaces in the Higher Education Sector. *Australasian Journal of Educational Technology*, 20(2) (2004): 232-247.

5   M. Ryan, Improving Reflective Writing in Higher Education: A Social Semiotic Perspective. *Teaching in Higher Education*, 16(1) (2011): 99-111.

I can reflect on a class that was not so successful). For me, the start of everyday reflective practice involves asking myself these two questions.

From this simple beginning, I then reflect on four specific areas drawn from the work of Benjamin Bloom and his colleagues:

1 Cognitive domain – what is thought, known and learned.

2 Psychomotor domain – the physical acts undertaken within the learning environment.

3 Affective domain – the emotions, feelings and beliefs that underpin the educational drive of all those involved in the learning environment.

4 Conative domain – the effort/endeavour of learning and teaching.[6]

These domains have clear and identifiable links to practice. In other words, I reflect on the content of the session and how well it was taught and learned. I reflect on my movement through the teaching environment and the body language of my students. I reflect on the relationships I have with my students and their interaction in the classroom. Lastly, I reflect on the effort that I put into my teaching and the effort that I feel they put into their learning. The following table shows some simple 'What?' and

---

6 B. Bloom, M. Englehart, E. Furst, W. Hill and D. Krathwohl, *Taxonomy of Educational Objectives: The Classification of Educational Goals. Handbook I: Cognitive Domain* (New York and Toronto: Longmans, Green, 1956); and D. Krathwohl, B. S. Bloom and B. B. Masia, *Taxonomy of Educational Objectives. Handbook II: Affective Domain* (New York: David McKay, 1964). See also E. Blair, Balanced Reflection as a Means of Practitioner Development in the Post-Compulsory Education and Training Sector. *Research in Post-Compulsory Education*, 16(2) (2011): 249-261; and E. Blair and A. Deacon, A Holistic Approach to Fieldwork Through Balanced Reflective Practice. *Reflective Practice*, 16(3) (2015): 418-434.

'So what?' questions that can be asked in relation to these four domains.

Cognitive domain	Psychomotor domain
● What was taught/ learned? ● Was there critical thinking? ● Was there analysis? ● What does this mean for my next teaching session?	● Did I move purposefully through the room? ● What was my body language like? ● What was my students' body language like? ● What does this mean for my next teaching session?
Affective domain	**Conative domain**
● What was my relationship with the students like? ● How did the students relate to each other? ● What does this mean for my next teaching session?	● How much effort did I put into my teaching? ● How much effort did they put into their learning? ● What does this mean for my next teaching session?

Everyday reflective practice is a tool for identifying areas of achievable change. The next step would be to enact this change. If we keep our targets focused and limited to the next teaching session (as opposed to grand targets that seek to make fundamental long-term changes) then we are more likely to implement them. Instead of seeing the development of teaching as a revolution, everyday reflective practice sees it as an evolution of small, implementable steps.

In becoming an everyday reflective practitioner, you need not start with reflection against the four domains outlined above, you could start with my two key questions: 'What?'

and 'So what?' Ask these questions after every session and make small changes in response to them. Then, as your practice develops, you could start adding to the process by reflecting on one or two domains. Over time you can draw in the other domains until you find yourself automatically reflecting and refining your teaching practice from a number of perspectives. In education, as in life, there is a lot of stuff that needs to be done and some of that stuff is tricky to do. Everyday reflective practice hopes to be straightforward and unencumbered – freeing up time for other, more onerous tasks, while slowly and purposefully enhancing the quality of our teaching.

In using models like the one on page 132, we can see that reflective practice is a means of self-analysis in order to examine our teaching practice – sifting out the good, the bad and the ugly aspects, and working out what works (and what doesn't). Rather than just walking out of a class-room and thinking, 'Yeah, that went OK today' or 'That was my best class yet and no one cried!' everyday reflective practice is a personal and analytical process. It is driven by reflexivity and a desire to improve, where intrapersonal examination leads to a modification in our actions, thoughts and feelings. Sometimes such a complicated process is easier to apply within a framework and some-times we need to consider our own position within such a framework. And this is where we turn to Vitruvius.

BALANCED REFLECTIVE PRACTICE

Marcus Vitruvius Pollio's major work, *De architectura* (c.30–15 BC), helped to define Roman architecture by expressing that buildings should be pleasing to the eye, should contain symmetrical features and should be built along specific proportions. This proportionate and balanced perspective is why Roman architecture and many of the neo-classical buildings that grace our cities are so pleasing to the eye. The ratio of a building's width to its height gives the appearance of things being balanced: the scale of the various arches seems just right and the columns are neatly set apart using mathematical formulae rather than just equal spacing. Later, Leonardo da Vinci drew on Vitruvius' work to develop a template for drawing the human body in proportion. His famous naked-man-in-a-circle, *Vitruvian Man*, shows the ratio of head to arms and legs to torso. The image shows that the span of a person's outstretched arms is actually the same measure as their height, offering a guide for artists who don't have da Vinci's talent. It is this balanced approach that I think we could draw on when developing an everyday reflective practice model.

Reflecting in a constructive manner is best facilitated by considering specific aspects of practice, rather than just assessing practice as one whole conglomeration of activity. Bloom's four domains offer us a proportionate and measured way to analyse practice at the personal level in a way that is easy to use. But that is only the start of the story.

The balance I have suggested is only really compelling when we take an objective position. If we look at stuff in a subjective manner then we can start to see our world in a very different way. For example, standing next to the fountain in the Piazza della Rotonda in Rome offers a fantastic view of the front of the Pantheon, which is about 50 metres away. From this distance, the huge isosceles-shaped roof sitting atop the portico columns is proportionate and satisfying. But as we move closer and sit on one of the steps, looking directly up one of the columns, the view becomes distorted. The same is true of da Vinci's *Vitruvian Man*. When we observe the drawing we see balance and proportion, but what if we *were* the Vitruvian Man? If we look through his eyes, and turn our head to look along one of our arms, there is a foreshortening effect – things that are closer appear bigger. What is objectively seen as proportionate can subjectively be seen as distorted.

When we observe the world we don't do so in an objective manner: we look through our own eyes and assess things using a mixture of our personal outlook and our environmental conditioning. This nature/nurture perspective means that reflection is value loaded, so what matters most to us takes on greater significance in our reflections. In this way our judgement of the world is foreshortened. Since we are subjective beings, a truly proportionate model of everyday reflective practice must embrace our humanity – balancing a framework for self-discovery with what we value. The question then moves from 'What should I reflect on?' to 'How does my personal perspective affect the things I reflect on?'

Everyday reflective practice is a conversation with ourselves that seeks to inform and develop future practice. It is a process for looking back over what we have done, examining the component parts and building a model for future teaching success. Using a framework that draws on the domains of practice, rather than unorganised reflections, can help in this process of becoming more focused. It can be further augmented through the development of a more personal dialogue where practitioners start examining the relationship between their reflections and the things that really matter to them as individuals. Reflection and self-awareness are important teaching skills, and having a personal and proportionate framework for examining practice might offer a resultant pedagogy that is pleasing to the eye, pleasing to our students and aligned with our individual values.

A REFLECTIVE CHALLENGE

● **Try to be balanced in your reflections.** Reflective practice without a reflective framework is merely 'thinking about stuff'. Reflective practice is not just about what you did. It's about examining why you did it: what was learned, how you feel and how you will grow. Reflective practice is a great tool for pedagogic development. Try reflecting on your cognitive, affective, psychomotor and conative traits. Make a habit of examining your teaching and the reasons behind your various successes and failures. Don't just rely on your overall gut instinct because that has very little utility. If we don't know why one class went well then it is very hard to repeat that success. Try to pick apart your practice along the domains outlined above. But be careful: humans have a tendency to dwell on the negative. Before you think about your weaknesses, consider the possibility that you have just improved someone's future. In balancing your reflections, start with one positive, then find one negative. Repeat this until you run out of positives – and then stop!

TEN BIG NUGGETS
TO REFLECT ON

1 **Students want to learn.** Over the years, the image of students has been corrupted and memes about them being lazy and switched off have crept into higher

education. Such ideas can lead to a faculty that is apathetic. Your conception of education should be current, active and relevant. It should resonate with your own passion for your subject and your own desire to learn. Understanding students as people who want to learn means that you need to reflect on how you stimulate their learning desires.

2 **Staff are there for students.** Modern higher education seems to have lost some of its focus and has become rather nebulous, with mixed ideas, ideals and goals. An overemphasis on producing world-class academic research outputs risks detaching higher education from its core function as a place of enquiry. It is time for teaching staff to realise the importance of developing teaching/learning relationships with their students and not to see their teaching duties as a distraction from their 'real' work. This relationship is symbiotic and there are many personal and professional rewards to be gained from supporting the learning experience.

3 **There is no room for lazy teaching.** The greatest teaching rewards in higher education result from effort and application. Teaching is an active process that involves planning and research, developing materials, fostering engagement and analysing knowledge. If higher education teachers take a laissez-faire approach to their teaching, they are likely to yield poor results and become indifferent about their practice. There is no room for lazy teaching in higher education: it fails to give proper regard to the subjects taught and it impoverishes the student experience. If you value your role in supporting your students' learning, then you are more likely to enjoy your work. Being a thoughtful and reflective teacher

makes the job more fulfilling, and it is 'easier' to teach when you feel part of such a virtuous cycle.

4 **There is no hierarchy of students.** There is a need to continuously reflect on how you are conceptualising your students, whether they are undergraduates, postgraduates, distance learners or part-time learners. Some higher education teachers perceive certain groups of students to be more 'important' than others, but this is an unhelpful mindset. Supporting the learning of *all* students is vital. If you are only interested in a certain subset, then you are opening yourself up to the charge of elitism and your teaching of other groups is likely to suffer. Students don't want, or deserve, to be taught by individuals who are elitist in who they would prefer to teach. It is important to remind ourselves that learning is a journey and we did not start at the top. Students sign up for courses in order to learn, so if we keep in mind that one of the key jobs in teaching is to help this learning, then we can remove false divides and develop a practice that is more egalitarian.

5 **It's not them – it's you!** There is nothing you can do about the make-up of the groups you teach, so consider how you relate to the students you do have, rather than the students you wished you had. If you are waiting for the perfect student or the perfect cohort, then you will be waiting for a very long time. Instead, reflect on how you can change in order to improve the learning of the students in front of you. Think about what you can do to better facilitate their learning. This might involve replacing materials, updating notes or changing the pitch and pace of your teaching, but it will almost certainly involve developing a more insightful understanding of the

learning experience and developing purposeful relationships with your students.

6 **Difficult concepts need simple explanations.** Some colleagues are guilty of overcomplicating their teaching, but complicated information is best taught in a structured and straightforward manner. In this way, the needs of the student are placed at the forefront and learning experiences move through logical steps so they can follow and build their understanding. Learning something new can be challenging, of course, but we need to actively examine the information we hope to pass on so that we do so in an intelligible way. There is little point in teaching a class if no one is able to grasp the content. We therefore need to develop feedback techniques (using students and peers) that enable us to gain an understanding of how successful we have been and whether we have made the learning accessible. Much of learning in higher education is difficult – and that's OK – but those of us who teach are responsible for making sure that we pitch our explanations of these tricky concepts at an appropriate level.

7 **You can't rely on others.** Ready access to a range of teaching materials makes it all too easy to use resources without examining them fully or personalising them. This can also occur when you find yourself teaching a course that has been planned by a colleague. Always aim to take a step back and scrutinise the resources, figure out what will work best for you and your students, and tailor the materials to your circumstances. Don't accept the research of others blindly or use materials without critical examination. Evaluation should take place before the teaching happens (in the planning stage), but it could also be incorporated into the teaching/learning

experience – the students could be encouraged to critically evaluate theoretical models. Pause whenever someone tells you they have already prepared the teaching materials for you: consider how their resources might relate to your educational philosophy, your teaching style and your cohort.

8 **Passion breeds passion.** In order for students to do well they need to have a sense of self-worth. They must feel that they are important players in the higher education system and that the subjects they study are valuable in some way. It is fulfilling for us as teachers to encounter students who are switched on and care about our subject. We have an important role to play: our students are more likely to be passionate about a subject if we show that passion in our teaching. Being enthusiastic about our subject is important in a number of ways: it makes for a more positive teaching environment, it is motivational, it encourages others to show a similar passion and it makes the job of teaching in higher education more enjoyable. Students come to university to learn, and it is easier to do so when they are in the right frame of mind. It is part of your job to make the learning as engaging as possible – and this can be done by being passionate about your subject.

9 **You are more important than the resources.** The move to online and blended learning alongside the increase in classroom technology has meant that tools such as podcasts, blogs and PowerPoints have become part of everyday practice. Those who teach in higher education need to scrutinise their use of such equipment and consider if they are using these tools to enhance their teaching or whether their teaching has become over-reliant on them. Here is a simple reflective question to consider: could you teach your

subject without electricity? This is not about rejecting technology, but rather emphasising the importance of the teacher as the fundamental conduit of learning. A genuine human connection and personal dynamic are more important than a screen full of support materials.

10 **If something is broken – fix it!** It is better to address issues rather than wait for them to fix themselves. Sometimes our teaching falls short of the standards we expect of ourselves. It is at this point, when we reflect back on a session, that we need to rework our materials. Too often we teach using the same resources year on year. There is no fundamental problem with this, as long as the content and pedagogy are refined and improved year on year. If this is not done shortly after a class, however, then key points will be forgotten and future improvements will be less focused. There may be times when it is clear that students don't quite 'get' an idea; if this is the case, rework the material so that future students do not encounter a similar barrier. The same is also true of student feedback systems (whether via committee or evaluation sheets): if students report that they would like improvements in a certain area, then it is vital that this is addressed in an open and constructive way. It can be difficult to hear negative feedback, but none of us is perfect and all of us can improve. Try to take time out to regularly reflect on what you have done to improve your teaching practice.

FINAL THOUGHTS

ACCEPT NOTHING

This book opened with the phrase, 'Question everything' and I still feel this is true. Look back over any key points you have found and consider how you might adopt or adapt these to develop approaches to suit your own particular type of teaching. You may have been intrigued by the wider conceptual discussions on the nature of teaching – what is it for and who is it for? Or you might wish to take some time out to reflect on what you think it means to be successful in teaching and in learning. But don't stop there. After reflecting, try to find a way of acting on your thinking. Ask 'What?' and 'So what?' to identify the ideas, tools and approaches that will work best for you, and then think about how you can actually apply them in your practice. Enacting some of the ideas presented here will come easier than others. For example, creating a three-part teaching session is a practical activity that I would urge you to start working on as soon as possible. Other concepts might take more time to act on – for instance, peer observation might be a longer term goal.

Nothing here is presented as a guaranteed winner – there are no universally agreed first principles in teaching. Teaching is a verb – it is about doing. Consequently, the only real way to measure the merits of the nuggets of wisdom (big and small) presented in this book is to make sense of them for yourself. Some of the nuggets are suggestions that you can easily implement, but others are designed as observations to stir your imagination and to help you create your own solutions to teaching problems.

Teaching in higher education can be a real joy. You are providing insight, skills and knowledge to the next generation. You are supporting individuals to become the best they can be. You are the start of the next part of their life's journey, so you have a responsibility to do your job to the best of your ability. This means moving beyond the old transactional model, where a teacher passes on knowledge to their students in exchange for their interest and awe. Instead, we need to shift to a new paradigm where engagement, excitement, discovery and analysis are placed at the centre of the learning experience.

REFERENCES AND FURTHER READING

Archer, L. (2008) Young/er Academics' Constructions of 'Authenticity', 'Success' and 'Professional Identity'. *Studies in Higher Education*, 33(4): 385–403.

Baggini, J. (2008) *Welcome to Everytown: A Journey into the English Mind* (London: Granta).

Bandura, A. (1997) Exercise of Personal and Collective Efficacy in Changing Societies. In A. Bandura (ed.) *Self-Efficacy in Changing Societies* (Cambridge: Cambridge University Press), pp. 1–45.

Barnett, R. (2000) *Realising the University in an Age of Supercomplexity* (Maidenhead: Open University Press).

Becher, T. and Trowler, P. (2001) *Academic Tribes and Territories: Intellectual Enquiry and the Cultures of Disciplines*, 2nd edn (Maidenhead: Open University Press).

Bell, M. (2001) Supported Reflective Practice: A Programme of Peer Observation and Feedback for Academic Teaching Development. *International Journal for Academic Development*, 6(1): 26–39.

Blair, E. (2010) Different Hefts, Different Expectations. *Learning and Teaching Update*, 39: 4–6.

Blair, E. (2011) Balanced Reflection as a Means of Practitioner Development in the Post-Compulsory Education and Training Sector. *Research in Post-Compulsory Education*, 16(2): 249–261.

Blair, E. (2018) Rebundling Higher Educational Research, Teaching and Service. *Confero*, 6(1): 35–54.

Blair, E. (2019) Mapping the Teaching Environment. *LSE Education Blog* (28 April). Available at: https://blogs.lse.ac.uk/highereducation/2019/04/28/mapping-the-teaching-environment.

Blair, E. (2019) What is a Lecturer? *New Vistas*, 5(1): 38–42.

Blair, E. and Deacon, A. (2015) A Holistic Approach to Fieldwork Through Balanced Reflective Practice. *Reflective Practice*, 16(3): 418–434.

Bloom, B., Englehart, M., Furst, E., Hill, W. and Krathwohl, D. (1956) *Taxonomy of Educational Objectives: The Classification of Educational Goals. Handbook I: Cognitive Domain* (New York and Toronto: Longmans, Green).

Boud, D. (2001) Using Journal Writing to Enhance Reflective Practice. *New Directions for Adult and Continuing Education*, 90: 9–18.

Bourdieu, P. (1988) *Homo Academicus*, tr. P. Collier (Cambridge: Polity Press).

Briggs, S. (2005) Changing Role and Competencies of Academics. *Active Learning in Higher Education*, 6(3): 256–268.

Busby, E. (2019) *Poorer Students Now Even More Likely to Drop Out of University Than Richer Peers, The Independent* (7 March). Available at: https://www.independent.co.uk/news/education/education-news/university-dropout-rates-students-rich-poor-education-a8812526.html.

Coates, H. and Goedegbuure, L. (2012) Recasting the Academic Workforce: Why the Attractiveness of the Academic Profession Needs to Be Increased and Eight Strategies for How to Go About This from an Australian Perspective. *Higher Education*, 64: 875–889.

Elkington, S. and Lawrence, L. (2012) Non-Specialism and Shifting Academic Identities: A Sign of the Times? *Innovations in Education and Teaching International*, 49(1): 51–61.

Foucault, M. (1986) Of Other Spaces [tr. J. Miskowiec]. *Diacritics*, 16(1): 22–27.

Gavin, L. A. and Furman, W. (1989) Age Difference in Adolescents' Perceptions of Their Peer Groups. *Developmental Psychology*, 25(5): 827–834.

Gordon, C. and Debus, R. (2002) Developing Deep Learning Approaches and Personal Teaching Efficacy within a Preservice Lecturer Education Context. *British Journal of Educational Psychology*, 72(4): 483–511.

Hattie, J. (2015) The Applicability of Visible Learning to Higher Education. *Scholarship of Teaching and Learning in Psychology*, 1(1): 79–91.

Henry, G. D. and Oliver, G. R. (2012) Seeing is Believing: The Benefits of Peer Observation. *Journal of University Teaching and Learning Practice*, 9(1), article 7.

Kinser, K. (2015) Working at a For-Profit: The University of Phoenix. *International Higher Education*, 28: 13–14.

Krathwohl, D., Bloom, B. S. and Masia, B. B. (1964) *Taxonomy of Educational Objectives. Handbook II: Affective Domain* (New York: David McKay).

Locke, J. (1997 [1689]) *An Essay Concerning Human Understanding* (London: Penguin).

Macfarlane, B. (2011) The Morphing of Academic Practice: Unbundling and the Rise of the Para-Academic. *Higher Education Quarterly*, 65(1): 59–73.

McKinnon, K. M. (2009) Adoration of the Mystic Lamb. In C. Gigliotti (ed.), *Leonardo's Choice: Genetic Technologies and Animals* (London: Springer), pp. 215–234.

Moon, J. A. (2013) *Reflection in Learning and Professional Development: Theory and Practice* (Abingdon and New York: Routledge).

Quinlan, K. and Åkerlind, G. (2000) Factors Affecting Departmental Peer Collaboration for Faculty Development: Two Cases in Context. *Higher Education*, 40(1): 23–52.

Ryan, A. M. (2000) Peer Groups as a Context for the Socialization of Adolescents' Motivation, Engagement, and Achievement in School. *Educational Psychologist*, 25(2): 101–111.

Ryan, M. (2011) Improving Reflective Writing in Higher Education: A Social Semiotic Perspective. *Teaching in Higher Education*, 16(1): 99–111.

Schön, D. A. (1987) *Educating the Reflective Practitioner: Toward a New Design for Teaching and Learning in the Professions* (San Francisco, CA: Jossey-Bass).

Schunk, D. H. (1991) Self-Efficacy and Academic Motivation. *Educational Psychologist*, 26(3–4): 207–231.

Williams, J. B. and Jacobs, J. S. (2004) Exploring the Use of Blogs As Learning Spaces in the Higher Education Sector. *Australasian Journal of Educational Technology*, 20(2): 232–247.

Wittgenstein, L. (1953) *Philosophical Investigations* (Oxford: Blackwell).

Yoshimura, Y., Sobolevsky, S., Ratti, C., Girardin, F., Carrascal, J. P., Blat, J. and Sinatra, R. (2014) An Analysis of Visitors' Behavior in the Louvre Museum: A Study Using Bluetooth Data. *Environment and Planning B: Planning and Design*, 41(6): 1113–1131.

978-178135337-0

978-178135338-7

978-178135339-4

978-178135340-0

978-178135341-7

978-178135373-8

978-178135353-0

independent thinking press

www.independentthinkingpress.com

INDEPENDENT THINKING ON MFL

MFL

Crista Hazell

HOW TO MAKE MODERN FOREIGN LANGUAGE TEACHING EXCITING, INCLUSIVE AND RELEVANT

HOW TO MAKE MODERN FOREIGN LANGUAGE TEACHING EXCITING, INCLUSIVE AND RELEVANT

CRISTA HAZELL

978-178135337-0

In the UK, MFL teaching has always had to battle with the 'everyone speaks English' argument, not to mention that, for so many, all that remains of their years learning a foreign language is *bitte, por favor or s'il vous plaît.*

But with teachers like Independent Thinking Associate Crista Hazell at the front of the class, things can be very different.

Drawing on her many years of experience as an MFL teacher and head of department, Crista shares tips, techniques and inspirational ideas geared to help teachers build confidence, increase enjoyment and improve outcomes as they take their MFL teaching to a whole new level.

Crista provides a range of strategies – from how to hook students in the minute they enter the classroom to ensuring that the vocabulary sticks – designed to help learners develop confidence, take risks and enjoy the challenge that learning a new language brings. She also offers ideas and advice on how to make learning new vocabulary and grammar a great deal more effective – and empowers teachers to open up the benefits and enjoyment of learning a language to all students, not just those in the top sets.

Ultimately, however, her book sets out to help teachers create engaging, relevant and memorable learning experiences in the MFL classroom and encourage their learners to become lifelong and passionate linguists.

For MFL teachers and heads of languages departments in primary schools, secondary schools and colleges.

INDEPENDENT THINKING ON RESTORATIVE PRACTICE

BUILDING RELATIONSHIPS, IMPROVING BEHAVIOUR AND CREATING STRONGER COMMUNITIES

978-178135338-7

MARK FINNIS

A practical and inspiring introduction to the use of restorative practice in schools in order to improve behaviour, foster a more caring culture and forge relationships that work.

For those educators who are uncomfortable with the punitive world of zero tolerance, isolation booths and school exclusions, Mark Finnis – one of the UK's leading restorative practice experts – is here to show you that there is another way.

Drawing on his many years' experience of working with schools, social services and local government across the country, Mark shares all you need to know about what restorative practice is, how it works, where to start and the many benefits of embedding it in any educational organisation that genuinely has people at its heart.

From coaching circles and the power of doing things 'with' (and not 'to') children and young people, to moving your values off lanyards and posters and into the lived experience of every member of the school community, readers will discover how restorative practice – when done well – can transform every aspect of school life.

INDEPENDENT THINKING ON TEACHING AND LEARNING

DEVELOPING INDEPENDENCE AND RESILIENCE IN ALL TEACHERS AND LEARNERS

JACKIE BEERE

978-178135339-4

Jackie Beere's *Independent Thinking on Teaching and Learning* is a practical guide full of educational wisdom to help teachers make a genuine difference to the lives of every young person in their classroom.

All the evidence shows that the most valuable asset in any classroom is the teacher at the front. No matter what changes are made to systems or to the curriculum, one certainty remains: children will be helped or hindered in their learning, job prospects, life chances and, indeed, happiness by the teachers they come across during their time in the education system.

In this all-encompassing book on teaching and learning, Independent Thinking Associate Jackie Beere draws on her many years' experience as a teaching assistant, primary teacher and secondary head teacher to re-energise every teacher's passion for their profession.

She champions both children and teachers as learners, and – together with expert advice on how to instil the habits of independent learning in all pupils – shares great practice that delivers outstanding outcomes for all educators.

Essential reading for all teachers and school leaders who wish to make an impact on the teaching and learning in their school.

INDEPENDENT THINKING ON TRANSITION

FOSTERING BETTER COLLABORATION BETWEEN PRIMARY AND SECONDARY SCHOOLS

DAVE HARRIS

978-178135340-0

When it comes to looking at the quality of our current schooling system, the biggest elephant in the room is transition. We do it the way we've always done it and, in so many ways and despite our best intentions, we often end up doing it badly.

But, as ever, there is another way.

Which is where Independent Thinking Associate Dave Harris comes in. With an impressive track record in leadership that includes establishing one of England's all-too-rare all-through 3–18 state schools, Dave knows first-hand how much can be achieved when all phases work together and keep the children, not the system, at the heart of all they do.

In this book he tackles school transition head-on, sharing a wealth of practical approaches and vividly illustrating how primary and secondary schools can better collaborate to ensure their pupils enjoy a smooth and effective move between the two phases.

Dave's passion for joined-up thinking between different phases shines through in his writing, as does his ingenuity when it comes to the design and delivery of programmes that work. He provides a clear explanation of the differences between transition and induction programmes, and also shares a comprehensive set of appendices in which he presents a range of materials to support the ideas put forward in the book.

Suitable for all school leaders – from heads of department and heads of year to head teachers and transition leads – in primary and secondary schools.

INDEPENDENT THINKING ON LAUGHTER

USING HUMOUR AS A TOOL TO ENGAGE AND MOTIVATE ALL LEARNERS

DAVE KEELING

978-178135341-7

Education is too important to be taken seriously: everyone in our schools – from the youngest learner to the, ahem, 'most senior' teacher – likes to laugh.

And beyond the many stress-busting and morale-boosting benefits that laughter brings on an individual level, the collective rewards of laughter in the classroom setting are also numerous – such as enhancing openness and teamwork, stimulating imagination and creativity and, above all, strengthening the student–teacher relationship.

No one is more familiar with the power of classroom conviviality than 'stand-up educationalist' and Independent Thinking Associate Dave Keeling, who in this book takes readers on an enlightening journey into the part that humour can play in improving the learning experience for all concerned.

Writing with his trademark wit, Dave shares handy hints acquired from his experience in the world of comedy and offers a veritable smorgasbord of activities for use with learners – all proven to generate laughter, enhance learning and make the teacher look great.

The teacher's mission, if they choose to accept it, is to take these ideas and exercises and adapt, enjoy, explore and generally mess about with them to their heart's content.

An inspiring read for all teachers and educators.

INDEPENDENT THINKING ON EMOTIONAL LITERACY

A PASSPORT TO INCREASED CONFIDENCE, ENGAGEMENT AND LEARNING

RICHARD EVANS

978-178135373-8

Independent Thinking on Emotional Literacy shares an approach that will help educators boost their pupils' emotional literacy, with the broader aim of nurturing a more grounded, engaged and intrinsically motivated child.

Do teachers truly understand their pupils? And do the pupils themselves really understand their own needs?

In *Independent Thinking on Emotional Literacy*, Richard Evans reminds every school educator that behind every child is a set of circumstances so entwined – and within them a set of emotions so involved – that to ignore them is to be complicit in any educational failings.

Richard's aim in this book is to help improve and harness both the educator's and their pupils' emotional literacy by promoting discussion around the often-unspoken issues that prevent children from making progress at school. He also shares with teachers a tailor-made passport template to start them on the road to deeper pupil understanding – whether it's for the girl who falls asleep at the back, the boy who needs constant support on a daily basis, or those pupils who'll need extra careful attention at parents' evening.

INDEPENDENT THINKING ON LOSS

A LITTLE BOOK ABOUT BEREAVEMENT FOR SCHOOLS

IAN GILBERT WITH WILLIAM, OLIVIA AND PHOEBE GILBERT

978-178135353-0

Written by Independent Thinking founder Ian Gilbert together with his three children, *Independent Thinking on Loss* is a personal account of the way educational institutions tried and succeeded, tried and failed and sometimes didn't try at all to help William, Olivia and Phoebe come to terms with the death of their mother.

Several months after their mother's death, BBC's Newsround aired a brave and still controversial programme in which four children talked about their losses. This prompted Ian and his children to sit down and think about their own experiences and draw up a fifteen -strong list of dos and don'ts that could help steer schools towards a better understanding of what is needed from them at such a difficult time.

The warmth of reception of this handout led the family to expand their advice and suggestions into what has now become Independent Thinking on Loss, the proceeds of which will go to Winston's Wish, one of the UK's leading children's bereavement charities.

Ian, William, Olivia and Phoebe encourage educators to view death and bereavement as something that can be acknowledged and talked about in school, and offer clear guidelines that will make a difference as to how a school can support a bereaved child in their midst. They also explore how conversations and actions – little ones, whole-school ones, genuine ones, professional ones, personal ones – in the school setting can make an awful scenario just that little bit easier for children to deal with.

independent thinking

Independent Thinking. An education company.

Taking people's brains for a walk since 1994.

We use our words.

www.independentthinking.com